Theological Violence in the 21st Century is a wide-angle lens look, a summary of events and conditions that have brought us to the present moment of confusion and angst in America. It is called "Theological Violence" because the book tracks a kind of wasting away of most, if not all, foundational principles that have held humanity upright for a very long time. It's violence because it is an assault on the foundations of faith while forging a new "faith context" paradigm based on theory, conjecture, postulation, and worse of all, out-and-out unbelief. In the midst of our current cultural confusion in America, the Church has been weakened and mostly anemic—largely complicit in the destruction of a moral life in our nation, her voice having been silenced as an ineffective witness. Scott's book maintains that only a penetration of the Word of God in the mind and heart of the individual will cause the calamity of our present environment to recede. The great bulk of the book skillfully lays out the penetration of the Word of God which will change the Church and position her for a "last days' witness."

—Mike Bickle
International House of Prayer of Kansas City

Dr Scott Kelso's examination of the twenty-first century Church—its curses and cure—is a must read for any Christian who senses the Spirit calling us into maturity and power. The new religion of secularism with its calculated dismantling of Christian virtues—the very glue that holds our America together—must be challenged by the power of the Gospel that Jesus introduced and on which St. Paul was centered (Romans 15:18–19). This can and must be done by just a little effort and a willing faith in the power of the Holy Spirit.

—Jon Ruthven
PhD Director, Iris University

I Just finished Dr. Scott Kelso's *Theological Violence in the 21st Century*. It is interesting drawing upon biblical, historical, political, and philosophical sources to consider where the Church is in our post-modern, post-Christian context. It is a book of hope and faith believing for a victorious climax to human history as it enters fully into the completion of the Kingdom of God. Scott gives us good advice on how to keep our faith in the midst of our materialistic culture, how to understand the true Judeo-Christian roots in the founding of our country and the Declaration of Independence. He takes up the subject of the validity of the prophetic in these especially troubling times. The book, however, isn't primarily about the USA; it is about the Kingdom of God and the Church of Jesus Christ in revival. It is a very interesting and timely read for such a time as this. For those who need light and hope in the midst of what seems to be darkening times, Dr. Scott Kelso will encourage you.

—Randy Clark
D.D., D.Min., Th.D., M.Div., B.S. Religious Studies
General Overseer, Global Awakening Apostolic Network
President of Global Awakening Theological Seminary

I am excited about Scott Kelso's new book *Theological Violence in the 21st Century: The Eclipse of Ethics and Morality in Today's World* for three primary reasons. First, Scott artfully describes the Church's current problems and issues in both an engaging and yet historically thorough way. Secondly, having known Scott for over twenty-five years, I know for a fact that Scott is not merely an armchair critic of today's Church problems. He has been a practitioner and a pioneer in the Church as a leader, relentlessly seeking first the Kingdom of God in the fullest sense. And as a leader who is both Word and Holy Spirit-based, Scott has fought the good fight in championing living for God according to God's ways, not according to whatever winds of popularity may be ravaging church pulpits. Lastly, Scott encourages us to look to God and His ways alone to see a move of God's Spirit, which will bring healing to the Church and healing to our nation and culture.

Scott gives us a call and necessary insights to see a favorite quote of mine realized once more in America: "*We do not want a church that will move with the world. We want a church that will move the world.*" G.K. Chesterton

—Marc Dupont
Mantle of Praise Ministries

Scott Kelso has been a key leader in educating the body of Christ to the supernatural power and work of the Holy Spirit. He has served in key leadership and teaching roles in and through Aldersgate Renewal Ministries, a ministry whose purpose is to encourage and equip the body to work and move in the power of the Holy Spirit.

Scott's new book *Theological Violence in the 21st Century* does a great job sharing the issue that has plagued the body of Christ in the past. It gives great insight on how we can move forward in raising the next generation to minister and move in the power of the Holy Spirit. Scott encourages Christ followers to move in and expect the supernatural on a regular basis to bring forth renewal and revival in the body of Christ.

Thank you, Scott, for your continued love for the body of Christ, for your encouragement for all of us to do the work of

Christ, not in our own strength but by the supernatural wisdom, guidance, and power of the Holy Spirit.

—**Mark Barrow**
Executive Director, Aldersgate Renewal Ministries
Goodletsville, Tennessee

The importance of biblical reflection, Holy Spirit thinking, and prayerful reflection cannot be marginalized. Leadership especially must encourage others by engaging together in these activities. In *Theological Violence in the 21st Century*, Scott adds his voice from experience by highlighting God's Word and the place of the Holy Spirit with his delving into the history of the USA. Here the reader too will find a helpful resource from across the Christian spectrum. May Scott's timely contribution further enable charitable discussion, critical thinking, and ongoing confidence in our Sovereign Lord Jesus.

—**Archbishop Sean Larkin**
United Anglican Church

As the Church faces a culture that is increasingly hostile to Christianity, Scott Kelso asks the questions: how did we get here, and what do we do now? In *Theological Violence in the 21st Century*, Scott reminds us that this is not the time for inaction or throwing in the towel but a time for the Church to be empowered by the Spirit, return to the fear of the Lord, and seek to be God's prophetic voice.

—**Dr. Michael Brown**
Host of the *Line of Fire* broadcast
Author of *Jezebel's War with America*

In *Theological Violence in the 21st Century*, Scott Kelso offers a strong critique of the tendency among churches to acquiesce to cultural pressure. We Christians too easily accommodate our teachings and ministries to the values of the present age, rather than rooting them in the values disclosed to us through divine revelation in Scripture. Kelso calls us to repentance. He invites us out of the chaos of the modern West and into lives of holiness in relationship with Christ.

—David F. Watson, Ph.D.
Sr. Vice President
Academic Dean and Vice President for Academic Affairs
Professor of New Testament
United Theological Seminary

THEOLOGICAL VIOLENCE IN THE 21st CENTURY

The Eclipse of Ethics and Morality in Today's World

Dr. Scott T. Kelso

Theological Violence in the 21st Century:
The Eclipse of Ethics and Morality in Today's World

© **Scott T. Kelso** 2021 All Rights Reserved

M E D I A
Distributed globally by Boss Media.
New York | Los Angeles | London | Sydney

Paperback ISBN: 978-1-63337-507-9
E-book ISBN: 978-1-63337-508-6
LCCN: 2021908956

Manufactured and printed in the United States of America

I dedicate this book to all the pastors who have remained faithful and true, who have persevered and not caved in to a post-Christian world culture.
Your reward awaits you.

—I Peter 1:3–5—

TABLE OF CONTENTS

FOREWORD

HOW AWARE ARE YOU OF WHAT is happening in your own culture? Often, we cannot see what is "hidden in plain sight." There is an old joke where one goldfish asks another, "How's the water?" The other fish replies, "What's water?" We the Church can be blissfully unaware of the nature of what surrounds us and how it influences us. God's people have always been influenced by their surrounding culture. This is inevitable and is not always a bad thing, but it often blinds us to reality and detracts or deflects us from being ardent followers of Jesus. Scott's book is a timely reminder of the dangers of the water we now swim in, particularly in North America. He believes that the answer to our love affair with modernity lies in the Bible, or more precisely, in the God the Bible proclaims.

Our own culture always appears, from the inside, to be self-evidently sensible, but history clearly demonstrates that in fifty or a hundred years' time, people will look back on us and think we were unenlightened. This book attempts to present us with such a critique today so that we can find an appropriate response.

In *Theological Violence in the 21st Century*, Scott traces the background to some of the trajectories that society has taken, particularly the influence of the libertarian 1960s, which rattles on down through the decades that have followed. It has been said that "The church that is married to the spirit of this age becomes a widow in the next." What now seems like the freedom to be ourselves will one day be viewed as a disastrous attempt to throw off common sense and reason. In the future, some of the current values we now hold dear will be seen as nothing more than bondage to ideologies which were misguided. Scott helps us reconsider several of the current trends in society against the backdrop of the Bible and 2,000 years of Church history.

Only by naming what is harmful can we thoroughly avoid it. The biblical prophets often provided a commentary on the situation of the contemporaries. Although he would not claim to be on a par with them, Scott has sought to do something similar for us today. He provides us with a lens through which to view society and the Church in North America. We all tend to follow the crowd, and it is likely that many of current political or religious loyalties, so fervently held as being "right," will one day be regarded merely as forms of early twenty-first century tribalism. Future Christians will see that many of us have embraced secular dreams in place of the Christian dream of a kingdom that is both near at hand and also coming. Perhaps we can name these trends now and change things for the better. Scott views the Church as the beating heart of society, perhaps unrecognized or marginalized, but the true source of hope. But we can only will be effective if we remain alert, or "awake" to use Scott's term. He rightly warns against any attempt to recapture a past Golden Age. Rather, we need to keep our eyes on the future and wake up to the fact that God's kingdom could arrive in its fullness at any time.

Dr. Richard Roberts
Leader of the New Charismatic Church group (UK),
Trustee of the International Charismatic Consultation (UK)
and Ffald y Brenin retreat centre, Wales

CHAPTER 1

MOVING THE ANCIENT BOUNDARY MARKERS

A HISTORY OF GOD'S PEOPLE IS ONE that narrates a struggle against constant erosion of fidelity to the living God. In the Bible, humankind begins with a revelation from God, "a thus saith the Lord" out of which God's servants react with their totality of being—spiritually, emotionally, and voluntarily.[1] The resulting imprint is so great that the revelation is then codified and written down.

In theological terms, we call this "inspiration." One can observe, for example, the need to record a pattern of impression going back in history twenty-five or thirty thousand years with humans marking their journey on the walls of caves throughout France and Spain. Man must record his journey. It is what we do. For the one in dialogue and covenant with God, first comes revelation then comes inspiration.

In the above context, the Bible is a record of God's journey with the human race written by over forty different people, many of whom never knew each other during a period of some three to four thousand years. Yet it provides a complete narrative with a beginning (Genesis) and an end (Revelation) and has guided countless individuals and numerous civilizations over time. Following this process, such things as rules, laws, mores, and other cultural markers are designed to help the group or tribe maintain allegiance to their revelation.

In addition, such things as memorials, rituals, monuments, statues, paintings, music, sculptures, and the like, motivate the new generation to follow the original ways given through revelation. An example is found in Joshua 4:4–7:

> So Joshua called together the twelve men he had chosen—one from each of the tribes of Israel. He told them, "Go into the middle of the Jordan, in front of the Ark of the Lord your God. Each of you must pick up one stone and carry it out on your shoulder—twelve stones in all, one for each of the twelve tribes of Israel. We will use these stones to build a memorial. In the future your children will ask you, 'What do these stones mean?' Then you can tell them, 'They remind us that the Jordan River stopped flowing when the Ark of the Lord's Covenant went across.' These stones will stand as a memorial among the people of Israel forever." (NLT)

As Archbishop (Philadelphia) Charles J. Chaput says in his book *Strangers in a Strange Land*, "Traditionally, nations depend on the continuity of generations to transmit memories and beliefs across time and thus sustain their identity."[2]

For some twenty centuries, the Church has been the custodian of such memories and beliefs. The process of erosion mentioned above can be readily observed in the last sixty years in America.

The cultural chaos today finds its genesis in a movement of young people known as the '60s revolution. Some reading this book have lived through and witnessed this radical intrusion into culture.

As a tracker employs markers in the woods to find his way back to his origin, we shall review markers that lead directly back to the 1960s upheaval when the Church abandoned its role in society to be salt and light, losing her mandate (commission) from the God of the Bible and caving in to a political correctness while at the same time leaving a great void in its wake.

This book is about reclaiming lost ground and reversing course before it is too late. Jesus made a haunting statement to His disciples on one occasion by saying "... work while it is day: for the night cometh, when no man can work" (John 9:4 KJV).

The Church in this hour is about to step into a prophetic role as an end times destiny calling which we will unpack later in this book. Because she has abdicated her allegiance to ancient revelation and is rewriting a new moral code, she has caused "theological" violence of sorts to engulf the religious landscape. This theological violence amounts to a kind of wasting away of most if not all foundational principles that have held humanity upright for a very long time.

It's violence because it is an "assault" on the foundations of faith while it forges a new faith paradigm based on theory, conjecture, postulation, and worse of all, out-and-out unbelief. Here we are reminded what the great nineteenth century preacher and expositor Charles Spurgeon asserts concerning those who denigrate the Word of God: "Many modern critics are to the Word of God what blow-flies are to the food of men; they cannot do any good, and unless relentlessly driven away they do great harm."[3]

The antecedent to this process of "wasting away" of foundational truths can be found in the historical/critical school of biblical interpretation of the eighteenth and nineteenth centuries scholastic world. This pursuit, which came largely out of Germany, left in its wake a pulverized landscape of conjecture, distorted reasoning, and out-and-out destruction of what has been an anchoring repository of faith understanding based on the authority of the Bible through the centuries.

One of the forefathers of this movement was Julius Wellhausen (1844–1908). He taught the Old Testament at the University of Greifswald. According to his theory, the Pentateuch (first five books of the Bible) consisted of four intertwined strands of documents that had been composed well after the exilic period (587 BC). The strands were identified as "JEPD." The "J" represents the proper name for God as revealed to Moses, known as YHWH (Yahweh); the "E" stands for the original Hebrew name for God—Elohim; the "P" represents the priesthood view of God; and the "D" stands for the Deuteronomistic history of Israel inclusive of the books of Deuteronomy, Joshua, Judges, 1 Samuel, 2 Samuel, 1 Kings, and 2 Kings.[4]

Wellhausen's theory is a forced narrative to explain how Israelite religion must have developed. In fact, Wellhausen resigned his position at Greifswald in 1882, realizing that "his theory was in compatible with his job of preparing students for Christian ministry."[5] Professor Corduan says, "By sending historical events to the margins of relevance, Christianity becomes pointless."[6]

In this, Wellhausen completely upends the history, the time lines, and the supernatural element in the prophetic ministry recorded in the Old Testament. The only bright spot in this episode is that Wellhausen had enough integrity to resign in the first place. In his book *In the Beginning God, he explains,*

I became a theologian because the scientific treatment of the Bible interested me; only gradually did I come to understand that a professor of theology also has the practical task of preparing the students for service in the Protestant Church, and that I am not adequate to this practical task, but that instead despite all caution on my own part I make my hearers unfit for their office. Since then my theological professorship has been weighing heavily on my conscience.[7]

As one can plainly see, drilling down on the wider dimensions of this effort to make the Bible say what it in effect does not say, one would be blind not to observe a breach in the traditional grounding of the people of God. Within this cauldron of intellectual suicide, the historical, critical school has embraced a worldview that no longer has room for the supernatural events of the Bible or the mystery of the living God. Just as the constant pounding of waves of water on the rocky, jagged ocean coast can render the rocks smooth over time, so the Church has mellowed over time to the relentless onslaught of the liberal theological academy. It has left a depleted foundation for the training of church leadership in our seminaries throughout the twentieth century.

To further illustrate my thesis, I refer to Dr. Donald E. Miller, a respected professor of the sociology of religion at the University of Southern California. He wrote a widely read book entitled *Reinventing American Protestantism: Christianity in the New Millennium*. The book was an attempt to understand the changing landscape of Protestant Christianity in the United States at the end of the twentieth century. Specifically, Dr. Miller set out to analyze three prominent church movements: Calvary Chapel, The Vineyard

Church, and Hope Chapel, all originating in Southern California. These movements had discarded many of the attributes of established religion (mainline Christianity) and were rapidly growing by connecting deep spiritual longings to contemporary cultural forms. By successfully "mediating the sacred," Miller has termed them the "new paradigm" churches, helping to re-energize a limping Protestantism into the twenty-first century.

In the introduction, Miller navigates an autobiographical segment where he admits writing a book twenty years earlier called *The Case for Liberal Christianity*. This book was "the product of a young mind trying to pick up the pieces from a graduate education in religious studies."[8] Then he really lowers the boom: "Most of my 'true believer' understandings of God and the Bible had been destroyed. In fact, I counted myself lucky to still consider myself a Christian."[9]

Miller admits shortly after the publication of *Liberal Christianity* "to shelve all attempts at writing theology until I was retired and had earned the right to engage in speculative reasoning. I had demythologized for myself most of the supernatural elements of Christianity and settled into the Social Gospel..."[10]

I too was educated under this paradigm of unbelief in 1970.

They have successfully dismantled the "faith of our fathers," leaving in their wake a disjointed and confused Church, who now records their individual distinction through branding (denominationalism). Thanks to the result of the Protestant Reformation, we have seen a fifty-year run on this kind of religious sequencing. This, in turn, has resulted in a depletion of resolve to address the very grand social and political problems which face our present-day society. Hence, Brandon Hatmaker describes the present-day Church as a river that is a "mile wide and three quarters of an inch deep."[11] He claims that "as our churches continue to grow in size, they lack in depth. Though our programs and events are becoming more and more broad, they only skim the surface of truth. Worse, critics contend, most believers don't actually live what they say they believe."[12]

Thankfully, the entire historical/critical apparatus has been rendered obsolete by many modern-day scholars. Unfortunately, the damage has already been done, and the Church has suffered greatly because of it. Please observe the following verification:

> One of the more dramatic developments in recent years in biblical and theology studies is the growing recognition of the obsolescence of the historical- critical method as an adequate paradigm for understanding the Bible. There is an increased awareness that the whole modern project's approach to the Bible was built on a faulty assumption of treating the text as object. Consistent with the assumptions of the modern project the quest of biblical studies focused on understanding the true historical context that gave birth to the final form of the text, and on clarifying the one univocal meaning that the text conveyed in this final form.

> Building on the work of Brevard Childs, who sought to understand the shape of the canon, and James Sanders, who sought to understand the process of the canon, numerous biblical scholars such as Walter Wink, James Smart, and Walter Brueggemann have all issued the same declaration that the focus of the critical apparatus was misdirected. They call instead for a serious treat-

ment of the Bible on its own terms, which translates into a rediscovery of its essential narrative character.[13]

In addition, the nineteenth-century abdication of biblical values led to a twentieth-century fundamentalist-modernist controversy, splitting the Church into two distinct camps, both of which shelved the supernatural of the Bible. Obviously, the modernists-rationalists approach abandoned the biblical witness to the supernatural a long time ago. This side of the equation may be dressed in clerical garb, but they are traitors through and through. As decedents of the Enlightenment, they could no longer conceive of a world where rationality was not king.

On the other hand, the fundamentalists led by B.B. Warfield, a nineteenth-century Calvinist theologian and self-described theologically as a "dispensationalist," believed that miracles and the supernatural were no longer needed after the canon of the Bible was complete. He based his entire approach (as well as those who followed him) on a verse in 1 Corinthians 13:9–10: "Now our knowledge is partial and incomplete, and even the gift of prophecy reveals only part of the picture. But when the time of perfection comes, these partial things will become useless." In this view, once the Bible was completed ("time of perfection"), there would be no more need for "additional" help through the supernatural gifts of the Spirit.[14]

Fortunately, this entire theological construct has been put to bed by a gifted theologian and friend, Dr. Jon Mark Ruthven, in a well-written book On the Cessation of the Charismata. Dr. Ruthven is the former chair of the doctoral program at Regent University in Virginia Beach and has authored several books on theological issues impacting the academy in recent days. In the above book,

Dr. Ruthven details a point-by-point rebuttal of Dr. Warfield's thesis, which has not to date been refuted by any sitting theologian anywhere. I highly recommend this book to the academy and the larger Body of Christ.

So, there you have it. Two sides of the same coin, heads and tails used to negotiate the fluid world of ideas about God and history.

Sadly, both groups were devoid of any power to contend with the oncoming giant of socialism and secular humanism unmasked in the 1960s revolution. By the time the '60s rolled around, the ground was fertile for a new crop of radicals to invade, and invade they did.

Because of these developments in theology and history, the Church by and large has relegated the Bible to a diminished role in society.

The Church has fallen in line with a politically correct (PC) agenda, genuflecting to the larger secular culture while it minds its place in a world gone mad. We have seen the Church subservient to cherished ideologies (political, theological, and social) and therefore have aided and abetted the theological violent confrontation between light and the darkness. How else, for example, could we allow homosexual marriage (Obergefell v. Hodges 2015) to be codified as an acceptable norm in America, overturning 5,000 years of human history?

A great mentor and a dear friend of the twentieth century, Dr. Lon R. Woodrum, said on one occasion, "There are a thousand roads that lead away from God, but only one road that leads back—repentance."

We would do well to observe Jesus's words to the Church at Ephesus recorded in Revelation 2:1–7. They had lost their first love and basically, Jesus admonishes us to "Remember your initial love. Repent and return, or else I will come and remove your lamp-stand (witness) from its place among the churches." I suggest from this perch of a diminished role in society, we have engendered a perfidious witness. We cannot, we must not let this stand.

MOVING THE ANCIENT BOUNDARY MARKERS

In a word, the Church finds herself in a grave predicament because she has chosen "to move" the ancient boundary markers of many core beliefs—a no-no for God's people in any age. It appears we have replaced these boundary markers with a kind of egocentric self-indulgent platform that has as its focus the maintenance of a conciliar status of comfort and consolation in a topsy-turvy world.

The status quo church seems to have lowered the bar to ac-commodate "seeker silhouettes" as I call them.[15] The idea is to make the local church as generic as possible so as not to offend those who may be curious about what goes on inside the building. After all, we are still counting nickels and noses.

The Apostolic Council I lead in Columbus has two African pas-tors who are under mandate from God to be missionaries to America. God knows we need it. When asked about their observation of Amer-ican pastors, one of them recently told us, "They fake it to make it," and "They are constantly playing to the audience to advance their position among the people they serve." Having locked themselves into a religious paradigm rather than a faith paradigm, they find them-selves compromised in their function of leadership. In a sentence, they soft-peddle the gospel to keep folks happy and comfortable.

However, if we return to the ancient boundaries (and super-impose them on our belief system), our vantage point will improve considerably. Let's take a look.

In the Old Testament, the boundary markers represented clear divisions of land ownership. The land supported the grazing of livestock, the growing of crops, and the livelihood of the owner. To fiddle around with them was a serious offence. The core rubric is found in Proverbs 22:28: "Remove not the ancient landmark which your fathers have set." It continues in Proverbs 23:10: "Do not remove an ancient landmark or enter the fields of the fatherless." In addition, Job weighs in when he says, "Evil people steal land by moving the boundary markers. They steal livestock and put them in their own pastures" (Job 42:2).

You see, the covenant cursed anyone who moved a boundary marker (Deuteronomy 19:14; 27:17), a curse reiterated by Hosea (Hosea 5:10). Those who had "inherited," not established the "ancient" boundaries, had no right to change what the ancestors had set up.[16] This understanding was accepted because the land was the Lord's, and the Israelites were merely His tenants (Leviticus25:23). Originally, the land was apportioned out by tribe—twelve tribes in all including the half-tribe of Ephraim and Manasseh. The land was His to apportion (Joshua 14–21). Moving a boundary marker stole not only property but crops. This loss could well ruin the life of a small farmer (Job.24:2–12, Jeremiah 50:34).

In the Bible, there is further injunction to confiscating the land of an orphan. The covenant includes warnings against oppressing or taking advantage of this group (Exodus 22:21, Deuteronomy 27:19, Zechariah 7:10–12). These people were particularly susceptible to oppression. The covenant provided for justice regardless of social class. An archetypical story of a violation of ancestral land is seen in Ahab's bloody appropriation of Naboth's vineyard (1 Kings 21).

Realizing America is not a theocracy, our democracy holds similar values and patterns of establishment from our founding fathers and founding documents, moving our boundaries only carefully and legally. These boundaries represent parameters within which we live. I am thinking of the Bill of Rights for example. We can add to them but only with two-thirds approval of Congress and three-fourths of the states voting by majority. A high bar indeed.

One clear area where we have moved the ancient boundary markers is with respect to our view of human life. We have cheapened and diluted the "sacred meaning" of life through the practice of abortion in America. Worse of all, we have codified it as the law of the land through our Supreme Court (Roe vs. Wade [1973]). Child sacrifice, being an ancient practice, has drawn the ire of a Holy God for centuries, especially among God's people.

Psalm 139:13 says, "For you formed my inward parts; you covered me in my mother's womb" (NKJV). Add to this Proverbs 24:11–12: "Rescue those who are unjustly sentenced to die ... Don't excuse yourself by saying, 'Look we didn't know.' For God understands all hearts, and he sees you. He who guards your soul knows you know. He will repay all people as their actions deserve."[17]

When one turns to the New Testament, one sees Jesus's attitude toward the most vulnerable of the population. One day, some parents brought their children for Jesus to bless them, but the disciples tried to interfere, thinking it was a distraction, but Jesus says, "Let the children come to me. Don't stop them! For the Kingdom of Heaven belongs to those who are like these children."[18] The Church is the custodian of the moral values surrounding life and the vulnerable. In effect, we have moved the ancient boundary markers concerning respect for human life and the most vulnerable by the practice of abortion.

In a brand-new survey done in January 2020 by the Cultural Research Center (CRC) of Arizona Christian University, George Barna, the most respected Christian pollster in America, says the survey has produced some very troubling conclusions.[19] The polling references four major groups: Evangelicals, Pentecostals and Charismatics, mainline Protestants, and Catholics. Most disturbing are the responses from the Evangelical end of the spectrum who traditionally have been the "bellwether" group espousing Orthodox Christian beliefs. Among the findings, 44 percent of the Evangelicals polled believed the Bible's teachings on abortion are ambiguous. In addition, 40 percent do not believe human life is sacred, 34 percent do not believe marriage is between one man and one woman, and 43 percent do not believe that God has a unified purpose for all people.

Barna admitted the numbers are not only alarming, they indicate "a post-Christian reformation" where Americans are redefining biblical beliefs according to secular values. This may result in completely upending every previously understood Orthodox understanding of the Christian mindset.

He concluded by saying, "It certainly seems as if the culture is influencing the church more than the church is influencing the culture."

How can this be in a nation where the vast majority believe in God and practice Christian faith? Indeed, we have some serious soul searching in the days ahead in America. I am reminded of a quote by A.W. Tozer in this regard: "In many churches Christianity has been watered down until the solution is so weak that if it were poison it would not hurt anyone, and if it were medicine it would not cure anyone!"[20]

To summarize this section, the spiritual boundary markers (inclusive of the entire Bible) are within which we are assigned to live our lives as believers in the living God. The obvious ones are, for example, the Ten Commandments (Exodus 20:2–17) (not ten suggestions for better living).

Jesus reduced these down to two; "love the Lord your God with all your heart, all your soul, all with your mind, and all your strength. The second is equally important: Love your neighbor as yourself. No other commandment is greater than these (Mark 12:30–31).

In the twenty-first century, as we keep whittling away at the broad stroke parameters for biblical living, we are at the same time losing credibility as a covenant people. In the following chapters we will attempt to remedy this dilemma.

CHAPTER 2

AN INHERITANCE OF THE '60S REVOLUTION

LET'S TURN OUR ATTENTION TO THE CATACLYSMIC decade of the 1960s. I have a particular affinity for this period of history—I lived through it. Following the riots at Kent State University on May 1–4, 1970, when four students were shot dead by Ohio National Guardsmen, a spirit of rebellion was released across many of the main university campuses across America. As Robert Ellwood says in his book on the '60s decade, "The 1969-1970 academic year was marked by unprecedented campus demonstrations and take over, mostly over antiwar and black power issues."[21]

I can remember sitting in my psychology class at Ohio State University with the jalousie windows open shortly after the events at Kent State. Student uprisings were taking place not far from the building I was in, and the tear gas was so strong, I could not see the blackboard because my eyes were watering so much. Picture this: I was not rioting; I was sitting in a classroom for crying out loud!

I knew at that point that I was not a part of the "change America now" crowd. I can remember very clearly saying to myself;

"This stinks! I'm paying for an education, and I'm being interrupted by a collective radical Marxist torrent."

Thankfully, I would be graduating in three months and moving on to my life's calling—Christian ministry. I had only been a Christian for less than a year, and I was interested in getting on with my life's work. My full testimony can be found in my book *Raising Up Biblical Eldership: Back to the Future with Spirit-Filled Leadership in the 21stCentury.*

THE DOWNWARD DIVE

Judge Robert Bork in his seminal book *Slouching Toward Gomorrah* begins with this comment on the very first page: "The long beast of decadence, a long time in gestation, having reached its maturity in the last three decades, now sends us slouching towards our new home, not Bethlehem but Gomorrah."[22]

You may recall that God in the Old Testament sent a fiery judgment on the two cities of Sodom and Gomorrah for their abhorrent sexual sin of debauchery and rebellion against God. Rebellions to the ways of God are not new to the pages of history and the 1960s certainly have their fair share.

Professor Bork supplies us with an adroit summary:

The Sixties combined domestic disruption and violence with an explosion of drug use and sexual promiscuity: it was a decade of hedonism and narcissism; it was a decade of which popular culture reached new lows of vulgarity. The Sixties generation combined moral relativism with political absolutism. And it was the decade in which the Establishment not only collapsed but began to endorse the most outrageous behavior and indictments of America by young radicals. It was the decade in which much of America's best educated and most pampered youth refused to serve the country in war, disguising self-indulgence and hatred of the United States as idealism. What W.H. Auden said of the 1930's was even more true of the 1960's: it was "a low and dishonest decade."[23]

Hillary Clinton declared at her 1969 commencement exercises: "We're searching for more immediate, ecstatic, and penetrating modes of living.[24] She saw this quest as religious as often as it was political or sexual or pharmacological.[25] Hence, the mantra of the '60s architects was "sex, drugs, and rock and roll" while their M.O. was "tune in, turn on, and drop out." In this matrix, the '60s music provided a constant soundtrack to change. This mindset was passed down through the youth culture as fast as COVID-19 today in a rock concert.

Some of the early architects of this dark descent were people like Norman Mailer (author/activist), Alan Ginsberg (Beat Poet), Susan Sontag (sexual liberationist), Eldridge Clever (the Black Panthers), Timothy Leary (the prophet of LSD), Charles Reich (author of *The Greening of America*), Norman O. Brown (author of *Life Against Death*), and Hannah Arendt (author of *On Revolution*).[26]

In addition, one of the well-known authors of the period was Theodore Roszak with his book *The Making of a Counterculture*. He thought the counterculture was an embryonic cultural base of the New Left "patterns, new sexual mores, new kinds of livelihood, new aesthetic forms, new personal identities on the far side of power politics, the Bourgeois Home, and the Protestant work ethic.

However, even he underestimated the appeal of the counterculture to be confined to a strict minority of the young and a handful of their mentors.[27]

The '60s history is simply too broad and deep to get into the weeds of this transformational movement. As Michael Anton wrote in his new book *The Stakes*, "Perhaps no era in the history of the world has been more analyzed, debated, chewed over, lionized, and (occasionally) criticized than America in the 1960s."[28]

So much has been written on the '60s legacy that we have an army of data to synthesize our conclusions. These include but are not limited to "government agencies and private foundations, research centers in and outside academia, social scientists and pollsters, professional journals, and even the daily newspapers produced a variety of statistics, surveys, analyses, polls, charts, graphs, ad tables that are the envy of historians working on more remote periods of the past."[29] The best we can do is only skim the surface in this chapter.

We are now left to sort through the rubble with one nation, but two cultures. "On one side originated in the traditional idea of republican virtue and the other emerged from a counter culture of the late 60's which has become the dominate culture of today."[30] Yes, we have had our share of countervailing groups such as the Moral Majority and the Christian Coalition in the '80s along with the Reagan Revolution. We have had the Promise Keepers in the '90s and the conservative Tea Party in the 2000s. These groups, however well-meaning, failed to dislodge the intransient hold of the '60s culture revolution.

One reason for the intransience is patience and persistence yoked with unity of purpose over a broad swath of American culture in successive decades. It actually is ironic that by the end of the '60s, "Their intense hope that religion, church and society were going to be deeply, radically changed within a few more years" came to an end.[31] "At some point in 1968 or 1969, they had to confront the reality that it was not going to happen."[32] However, upon graduating from college "they went into politics, print and electronic journalism, church bureaucracies, foundation staffs, Hollywood careers, public interest organizations, anywhere attitudes and opinions could be influenced."[33] And it is here that Roger Kimball names his book and their embeddedness *The Long March*.

Over time, the inheritance of the '60s would witness "incremental" deterioration of traditional American values and processes. As a society we would lament for a brief time and then become accustomed to it. We see the same thing today with the Democratic push for the Green New Deal; illegal immigrants voting rights; defunding the police; political correctness run wild; sanctuary cities; Antifa agenda tactics; Black Lives Matter doctrinal stance; and on and on it goes. Each of these new initiatives with their ideology in tow could adopt the slogan "no limits" as Francis Fukuyama as suggested.[34]

HOW DID WE GET HERE?

I suppose we could ask the broader question of how we got here in the first place. Sean Hannity in his new book *Live Free or Die* goes into some detail on the underpinnings of the '60s revolution. He suggests that we look at the first two decades of the twentieth century when at that time, journalists, novelists, political scientists, social scientists, poets, and others were riding a degree of momentum from their previous generation.[35]

By the time the industrial revolution was in full swing, capitalism and wealth inequality were glaringly present throughout the society. Freedom and free enterprise were proleptically on the move, while the progressive social justice devotees did not subscribe. In their minds, the government should seize control of the economy and suppress individual freedom so as to redress inequities of those less fortunate. The problem is that "socialists constantly exploit the poor as a pretext for accumulating more power for themselves and confiscating more of society's wealth for their own ends."[36]

The crux of the progressive philosophy worms its way back to the beginning of the Republic. This is precisely because "the progressives rejected the founder's belief in, and the biblical teaching on, the depravity of the human condition, believing instead that people are essentially good and perfectible, and that evil resulted from imperfect social systems and corrupt institutions that were impeding man from reaching his true potential."[37]

This is exactly where the '60s equation came out with respect to the Vietnam War and Civil Rights. These '60s geniuses didn't believe in personal liberty flowing from God-given rights as detailed in the Declaration of Independence. Their belief was and still is that government bestows rights and engineer's people's destiny by what is expedient from state interests.

> We may call it the perfection of humanity; the civilization of the world; the perfect development of the human reason, and its attainment to universal command over individualism; the apotheosis of man … The national state is the most perfect organ which has yet been attained in the civilization of the world for the interpretation of the human consciousness of right. It furnishes the best vantage ground as yet reached for the contemplation of the purpose of the sojourn of mankind upon earth.[38]

I like the way Professor Ronald Pestritto of Hillsdale College puts it: "Progressives sought to enlarge vastly the scope of the national government for the purpose of responding to a set of economic and social conditions, that, it was contended, could not have been envisioned during the founding era, and for which the Founders' limited, constitutional government was inadequate."[39] Therefore, in the grand scheme of things "The progressive movement thus chipped away at the founders' ideal of equal of *opportunity* under the law in favor of equality of *outcomes*."[40]

To be fair, we must dig a little deeper to fully comprehend the Left's agenda as it has morphed over the decades. To begin with, the "cornerstone of the sixties is civil rights—the effort to end Southern segregation, outlaw discrimination, and fully integrate American Blacks into every aspect of American life."[41] So far, so good. We must therefore, "bring within the pale of the constitution and civil society those who had hitherto been marginalized or excluded."[42]

Because the disadvantage has been so great over so long of a period of time, we are not just talking about "basic rights" such as living toward "all men are created equal" or even "judging everyone according to the content of their character, rather than the color of their skin." Even though these are noble core values, they do not go far enough to redress the wrongs and the "systemic inequality" that has been so intransient in our national institutions, our cultural apparatus, or our educational and economic enterprises.

During President Lyndon Johnson's commencement address at Howard University in 1965, he declared, "We seek not just freedom but opportunity. We seek not just legal equity but human ability, not just equality as a right and a theory but as a fact and equality as a result." [43] In other words, genuine equality requires equal outcomes.

This is why Professor John Rawls wrote in his massive book, A *Theory of Justice*, "All social primary goods—liberty and opportunity, income and wealth, and the bases of self-respect—are to be distributed equally unless and unequal distribution of any or all of these goods is to the advantage of the least favored."[44] This goes well beyond the Framers yet not far enough for later generations of the Left.

In our day, the Left has redefined "the favored" (e.g. white, favored, advantaged) to "the privileged" who are by contrast a group who are "inherent, undeserved, unearned, even somehow unnatural."[45] This, in turn, leads to an inherent oppression of the minority class in society by the "privileged" (subconscious, structural, embedded white America).

> But once "advantage" is redefined as illicit "privilege,"
> and "disadvantage" as resulting solely from oppression—
> and especially once past oppression is accepted as a cause
> of present disadvantage—then justice ceases to be a mat-
> ter of fairness to individuals but instead becomes a mat-
> ter of group redress.[46]

So, one could say the disadvantaged as a group become at this point, plaintiffs in a societal class action suit. I believe these to be Utopian directives, ever in pursuit, but never ultimately realized and which opens up an endless confrontation between the privileged and the oppressed. In addition, as each generation carries the struggle a little further, continuing to "reinterpret" as they go, a satisfactory conclusion will never be attained. Given the downward bent of human nature, one should not be surprised.

THE CHURCH AND SOCIAL WITNESS

As we launch into a discussion of the role of the Church in the '60s cultural upheaval, I believe that the cumulative effect of the sordid inheritance from this period as well as even the last fifty years shadows a church in a spiritually weakened and compromised condition. The Church has been morally compromised as Roger Kimball warns in his book *The Long March*, "… under a spiritual anesthesia of sorts."

There is no other way to describe it other than the Church has been laying down on the job, avoiding the needed confrontation with a decadent social atmosphere. Our mandate from Jesus Christ at any given period is to be "salt and light" in the culture (Matthew 5:13–14).

We represent another world, and our witness will be antithetical to the present. (More on this later.) What happens when salt loses its saltiness? Well, we have been finding out well over a generation now. However, before we drill down too far on this question, I believe it would serve us well to go back and read the most-read document in American history other than the Declaration of Independence and the Constitution. What is that document? It's called *Democracy in America* by Alexis de Tocqueville.

De Tocqueville was a French aristocrat commissioned by France to travel to America to study prison reform in the new land. Along with his friend Gustave de Beaumont, the two sailed from Le Havre, France and landed in Newport, Rhode Island in the year

1831, to begin what would be a two-year immersion in American culture from end to end. De Tocqueville cautions,

> A great democratic revolution is taking place in our midst; everybody sees it, but by no means everybody judges it in the same way. Some think it a new thing and, supposing it an accident, hope that they can still check it; others think it irresistible, because it seems to them the most continuous, ancient, and permanent tendency known to history.[47]

In fact, "the future of western Europe and North America, he insisted, belonged, for good or ill, to democracy. And that future, he believed, was sanctioned by the blessing of God."[48]

In light of this truth, it would serve us well to refresh our understanding of exactly what kind of culture de Tocqueville found in America that caused him to go way beyond prison reform. Consequently, the following quotations will suffice.

No better place to start than at the beginning. "Upon my arrival in the United States, the religious aspect of the country was the first thing that struck my attention; and the longer I stayed there, the more did I perceive the great political consequences resulting from this state of things, to which I was unaccustomed."[49]

He continued. "In France I had almost always seen the spirit of religion and the spirit of freedom pursuing courses diametrically opposed to each other; but in America I found that they were intimately united, and that they reigned in common over the same country."[50]

Please note, as we continue with this series of quotations, when de Tocqueville refers to "religion," he is talking about Christianity. It is not a generic term in this context.

De Tocqueville admits to being Roman Catholic, but when comparing Catholicism to the other branches of "religion" in the new world, he makes this amazing statement: "I found that they differed upon matters of detail alone; and that they mainly attributed the peaceful dominion of religion in their country, to the separation of Church and State. I do not hesitate to affirm that during my stay in America, I did not meet with a single individual, or the clergy or to the laity, who was not of the same opinion upon this point."[51]

He then drops this bomb: "In the United States the sovereign authority is religious, and consequently hypocrisy must be common; but there is not a country in the whole world, in which the Christian religion retain a greater influence over the souls of men than in America; and there can be no greater proof of its utility, and of its conformity too human nature, than that its influence is most powerfully felt over the most enlightened and free nation of the earth."[52]

De Tocqueville continues to weigh in on the vitality of Christianity as it relates to political considerations. He says, "I do not know whether all the Americans have a sincere faith in their religion; for who can search the human heart? But I am certain that they hold it to be indispensable to the maintenance of republican institutions."

This opinion is not peculiar to a class of citizens or to a party, but it belongs to the whole nation, and to every rank of society.[53] And of course, innate to any discussion of democracy is the concept of liberty. When President George W. Bush spoke to the National Endowment for Democracy in Washington shortly after the 9/11 attack on the World Trade Center, he said this about liberty: "We believe that liberty is the design of nature; we believe that liberty is the direction of history. We believe that human fulfillment and excellence come in the responsible exercise of liberty. And we believe that freedom—the freedom we prize—is not for us alone, it is the right and capacity of all mankind."[54]

Since liberty is so basic to everything American, de Tocqueville weighs in: "The Americans combine the notions of Christianity and of liberty so intimately in their minds, that it is impossible to make them conceive the one without the other; and with them, this conviction does not spring from that barren traditionary faith which seems to vegetate in the soul rather than to live."[55]

And finally, Charles Chaput puts a cherry on top of this sundae: "Tocqueville saw that the strength of American society, the force that kept the tyrannical logic of democracy in creative check, was the prevalence and intensity of religious belief. Religion is to democracy as a bridle is to a horse.

Religion moderates democracy because it appeals to an authority higher than democracy itself."[56] We could go on with scores of pages with such quotes. However, I believe that history speaks for itself.

Our democracy and our freedom with liberty have served us well for 244 years. However, reading Cal Thomas's new book *America's Expiration Date*, my confidence has been shaken by his thesis that says, "The average age of a nation or empire's greatness is 250 years."[57] Thomas was quoting Sir John Glubb, a career British soldier who led and trained from 1939 to 1956 and who wrote a book entitled *The Fate of Empires and Search for Survival*. Thomas had reviewed Glubb's intense study of major empires over the last 3,000 years and where Glubb had come to the conclusion that the average age of a nation or empire's greatness is 250 years. If that is so, could America be in store for a major correction on July 4, 2026?

THE CHURCH BETWEEN GOSPEL AND CULTURE

"The American culture has moved miles from the assumption of the Founders."[58] Madison and Hamilton wouldn't recognize us today and neither would Alexis de Tocqueville. It would seem the Church is embedded in a culture that is wholly alien to its constitution while the '60s have come home to roost.

James Hitchcock defines culture as "the totality of the life of a people, shaped and guided by their institutions but also to some extent a spontaneous development from the people themselves—their moral and religious beliefs, their social customs, their attitudes toward each other ... their sports and games, their community mores and many other things."[59] Knowing this, we acknowledge that culture and politics are first cousins. Someone said that politics is the practical application of deeply held values, for the most part being shaped by religion. Every culture will reinforce someone's values. It is the place of the Church to set the standards or at the very least be a part of the mix. Proverbs 29:2 (RSV) says, "When the righteous are in authority, the people rejoice; but when the wicked rule, the people groan."

I can't help thinking that if the Church had adopted Martin Luther King's values during the '60s struggle for justice against the entrenched by-products of slavery, we would not be in the situation we are in today, especially during the summer of 2020 with the destruction of Portland and Seattle. Listen to what Dr. King stated prophetically to a waiting world during their tumultuous hour of history, and judge for yourself.

> As you press on for justice, be sure to move with dignity and discipline, using only the weapon of love. Let no man pull you so low as to hate him.

Always avoid violence. If you succumb to the temptation of using violence in your struggle, unborn generations will be the recipients of a long desolate night of bitterness, and your chief legacy to the future will be an endless reign of meaningless chaos. (Martin Luther King Jr. 1956)

Darkness cannot drive out darkness; only light can do that. Hate cannot drive out hate; only love can do that. Hate multiplies hate, violence multiplies violence, and toughness multiplies toughness in a descending spiral of destruction—The chain reaction of evil—hate begetting hate, wars producing more wars—must be broken, or we shall be plunged into the dark abyss of annihilation. (Martin Luther King Jr. 1963)

And finally, during his Nobel Prize acceptance speech, in Stockholm, Sweden in 1964, he said,

One day we must come to see that peace is not merely a distant goal we seek, but that it is a means by which we arrive at that goal. We must pursue peaceful ends through peaceful means. Love is the only force capable of transforming an enemy into a friend.

Now that, my friends, you can take that to the bank! Let us for a moment superimpose these thoughts on the summer of 2020 following the tragic and heartbreaking death of George Floyd on May 26, 2020, where protests broke out in 140 cities across twenty-one states in our nation. Gatherings that began as a cause to fight justice quickly became overshadowed by rioting, theft, looting, and violence. The unjustified death of one man rapidly multiplied into countless additional deaths and hospitalizations along with billions of dollars' worth of damage. It is now estimated that the civil unrest from the tragedy on May 26 will likely go down as the costliest in U.S. history. My heart breaks as we as a society eschew Dr. King's vital words of life and plow on in our insouciant way.

The problem is the Church has painted herself into a corner. She has been in a process of "re-inventing" itself ever since the 1970s, realizing that the free ride is over, and it was late to the dance. Leslie Newbegin says in his book *Foolishness to the Greeks,* "The church finds herself in a pagan society, and its paganism, having been born out of the rejection of Christianity, is far more resistant to the gospel than the pre-Christian paganism with which cross-cultural missions have been familiar."

Ouch! So the culture was once our ally. Church and culture were aligned—e.g. prayer in schools, Bible reading, major institutions reinforcing Judeo-Christian values. But now the culture has decided to live godlessly and is collectively secular. The Church represents little enclaves of Christian faith in a pagan environment. This present culture in which the Church lives is in most ways antithetical to the life, teachings, and gospel of Jesus.

Because of these and many other factors, the contemporary Church continues to suffer "dry rot." She has lost moral authority over the last generation with her delinquent shepherds (Isaiah 56:10–11). Previous generations had their Jim Bakkers and their Jimmy Swaggarts. We have had our Trillian Tchividjians (Billy Graham's grandson) and our Ted Haggards and Todd Bentleys. And don't forget the Catholic Church with their superstar Cardinal Theodore McCarrick along with dozens of other priests who are still in litigation for sexual abuse of children under their purview. With each abysmal deluge, the Church at-large loses moral authority. "Christianity's moral norms are based on the idea that there is a way people are meant to function in the world."[60]

We seem to have shelved that concept. I heard a preacher-friend say recently, "God cannot be the source of your strength when the world is the source of your standards."[61]

There is no question, the Church in America is facing strong headwaters as she attempts to navigate present culture. Given the current COVID-19 crisis, the Word that many prophetic people throughout the Body of Christ are getting today is "RESET." In other words, we will not go back to church as normal or life as normal as before. Many things will change permanently in the wake of this health crisis.

Change is not always a bad thing. The Bible is full of corrective measures to bring people back on course. Perhaps just maybe God is up to something very unusual, and no one will see it coming. The COVID pandemic is a prime example. Never before in the history of the world has the entire planet "shut down."

Strap yourselves in, friends. It's going to be a wild ride to the conclusion.

CHAPTER 3

DISCERNMENT IN AN AGE OF RELATIVISM

THE WORLD IS LOST IN A DELUGE OF SIN AND INIQUITY. Has it ever not been that way? However, today the major forces that govern our society seem to be complicit in this swirl of darkness and confusion. Consider some of the forces we have to navigate each day just to live our lives: humanism—the casing that holds the cheese; unenlightened world wisdom (Proverbs 29:25); educational systems that virtually ignore God; elite media slanted toward pleasure, personal freedom, materialism, and sexual exploration; false philosophies of modern thinking such as evolution, homosexuality, abortion, and pornography as rights under our constitution; blind devotion to science and reliance on observable phenomena; proliferation of counterfeit religions, cults, and the occult; worldwide revolts against law and authority; sexually saturated music videos to capture the minds of our young people; bloodletting video games for conquest for our young children; and if this isn't enough—Harry Potter being the best-selling series in the history of publishing.

So as we launch into this chapter, perhaps the most important in this book, we will negotiate the importance of the mind through a process known as "discernment." The area of our thought life is a real struggle for any people. It is the devil's playground. If he can trap you there, he can immobilize you in the progress of your Christian walk.

We must remember that his accusations, his suggestions, are all based on lies, half-truths, and twisted and deceptive logic. We defeat him when we know the truth and walk in the truth.

Our minds are a battleground pure and simple. That is why the Scripture says to "study to show thyself approved" while Psalm 1:2 says "… and on this law he meditates day and night" and Romans 12:2 says, "And be ye transformed by the renewal of your mind …" (KJV). These are disciplines that actually help us walk in the fear of the Lord. If a person does not have some regular regimen in the Word of God, they will be easy picking for our arch enemy. If you don't know the book, you will be out of your weight class when wrestling with the powers that be.

Allow me to make this declaration: when a person gets saved, there is a Titanic turnaround in the area of the thought life. For the person who is dead-in-earnest with God, the mind has to be changed. When the thought life is under the governance of Christ, the thinking processes are altered from the natural-born state.

I want us to understand from the outset that what comes to us as a result of our reconciliation with God is truly astounding. When one comes to Christ, there is something that is added to their life, their experience, and their identity that is so powerful. It cannot be un-added in any subsequent future.

THE BATTLE GROUND OF THE MIND

One reason the mind is a battleground is because it is like a giant sieve. Everything goes through it unless you are asleep, and then it is still active albeit at a different level.

Think about it. The complexity of modern society and the impute of the mass media, put enormous pressure on our thought patterns. Life is no longer a simple process of growing up gently amid a small circle of family and friends. No, today the trouble, the turmoil, the tragedy, the tension of the entire planet is dropped onto our doorstep and thrust into our lives.

Just today I received the news alert on my phone: "Wedding guest in Texas shoots groom in chest; bride refuses to talk."[62] Every day, we are bombarded with threats of terrorism, road rage, home invasions, and accidents of all kinds, weather disasters, and on and on. We are deeply enmeshed in the hardship and heartache of the entire human family. On the outside, a person may give a pretense of poise and calm, while on the inside, they are engulfed in a violent struggle, terrible thoughts, evil imaginations, fantasies, and every form of twisted thinking.

When one adds to this the doled-out pablum that's being passed off as the Gospel in many of our Christian churches, but it does not really remotely resemble the New Testament Gospel, well, the Church is under a real challenge in our day. Thank God we have a reserve in Christ to counteract the dark and demonic delusion of this world.

Isaiah 55:7 (RSV) says, "let the wicked forsake his way, and the unrighteous man his thoughts; let him return to the Lord, that he may have mercy on him, and to our God, for he will abundantly pardon."

Let us be clear. All sin begins in the mind. Proverbs 23:7 says, "For as he thinketh in his heart, so is he ..." (KJV). David says in Psalm 51:6, "Behold, thou desirest truth in the inward being; therefore teach me wisdom in my secret heart. (RSV). This is, of course, the area of the thought life. The person, who commits acts of immorality begins with lust in the mind or the secret heart. Psalm 111:10 (RSV) says, "The fear of the Lord is the beginning of wisdom; a good understanding have all those who practice it. ...."

Some people have the idea that our thought life is a private sanctuary and nobody's business but ours. And anyway, thinking wrong thoughts is not nearly as bad as doing wrong deeds. This is not true. Proverbs 15:26 says, "The thoughts of the wicked are an abomination to the Lord, the words of the pure are pleasing to him." Our thoughts sound as loudly in heaven as our words do on earth.

Ouch! Some may ask, "How can I possibly control this?" It becomes a process but Colossians 3:2 records, "Set your minds on things that are above, not on things that are on the earth." As we yolk this with James 4:7, "... Resist the devil and he will flee from you," we will see results.

So in contrast to the false ideologies, teachings, and lifestyles of this present degenerate and dark world (Philippians 3:19), we find in Scripture simple guidelines for victory in this area of our lives. It is called "discernment."

A HEART TO DISCERN

Ezekiel lifts up a major priority of God for his people in all time who are in covenant relationship. He wants them to develop an antithetical posture of living (countercultural). This involves the distinction between the clean and the unclean, between the holy and the common.

Here is the mandate the Levitical priesthood will follow in teaching a faithful remnant in Israel: "They shall teach my people the difference between the holy and the common, and show them how to distinguish between the unclean and the clean" (Ezekiel 44:23). This becomes the fulcrum of this chapter. There are corollaries throughout Scripture to this injunction.[63]

God's purpose was to alert the Jew to the fact that all day long, every day, whatever he does, he must consciously choose God's way. This would include choices about food, clothing, farming techniques, justice, health care, holidays, patterns of worship, and others.[64] Now, given many of these followed ceremonial procedure linked to religious law (Leviticus 10:10), of which we are no longer under today, however, this whole area was designed by God to develop in us an antithetical mentality (countercultural). And that is still the heart of God. Granted this was ceremonial procedure linked to religious law.

However, the spirit of it is still intact. (See Chapter 7: Form and Essence.) The ceremonial law is gone for us, but the moral law is intact for all.

The Jew was literally to go through life distinguishing God's ways from those which were not God's ways. You may ask, "Why do I need such measures of discernment in the Age of the Holy Spirit? Is it not the Spirit's job to guide us?"

Yes, but it is also the age of every other spirit. Evil, deceiving spirits, are dispatched on mankind with increasing intelligence because the time is short. Just because you are a Christian and moving in the Holy Spirit does not mean that discernment is automatic. God's ways have to be learned. They cannot be discerned if they are not first learned (e.g., Hebrews 5:11–14).

Think with me the extent to which the boundaries have been erased in our culture today. It literally is "anything goes" as long as you are not breaking the law or hurting someone.[65] And even then, it is not observed.

So here is the onus for the discerning disciple living in the twenty-first century: discernment is the *"divinely given ability to distinguish God's thoughts and God's ways from all others."*[66] Proverbs 16:21 (NIV) says, "The wise in heart are called discerning, and gracious words promote instruction."

May I say at this point, people all through history have developed spiritual regimens which include various "directives" designed to help one pursue the interior life of the Spirit and thereby, be able to track progress in a positive direction. St. Ignatius of Loyola is one such example. Ignatius lived from 1491 to 1556. He was the founder of the Society of Jesus (Jesuits), a Catholic order not only characteristic of the pursuit of the interior life in the Spirit, but also active in the culture through sociopolitical involvement.

Much could be said about St. Ignatius' contribution to Christian history, but his authorship of a book entitled *Spiritual Exercises* has helped millions discern the path to inner wholeness and well-being through the discernment of spirits. His fourteen rules for the pursuit of the inner life are classic in the Catholic world. In his book on Ignatius, Father Timothy Gallagher says, "If our spiritual tradition can offer us an instruction capable of permitting us also to live our daily lives with discernment, then that tradition is offering us an invaluable treasure."[67]

When in pursuit of such a tradition or directive, "the persons so aided are increasingly enabled to make a spiritual sense out of their experience, and so to live ever more attuned to the Lord's will. That is the goal of all discernment."[68]

As we continue, we will see it as the Holy Spirit's job to make us "aware" and thus open the gateway to all discernment.

CONTINUUM THINKING

Many people today have not grown up being taught the Word of God—realizing the contrasts that exist between God's ways and all others. Most in the Church in America have not committed to an intensive study of the Bible, although they come to church every week and live descent lives and are known as Christians. In addition, these people have been schooled by modern educational systems, newspapers, magazines, radio, TV, and the Internet to the extent that all they really know is continuum thinking. In this, we don't realize how pervasive the culture is on our thinking and conduct.

What is continuum thinking? Essentially, it is defined as "in every idea, there is a shade of gray. There is not right or wrong, true or false, only shades of right or wrong, true and false spread along a continuum. The poles are so far out on the wings, for all practical purposes, they are unattainable. Nothing then is wholly right or wrong."[69]

In education, this is known as "values clarification," and in religious circles, it is called "situation ethics," another gift from the '60s. Today, we see one of the most popular books on the market in the last few years is called *Fifty Shades of Gray*. It is all about sexual promiscuity while the lead character is named Christian. Go figure!

But if you are a serious student of the Word of God, you will think in terms of contrasts. —What it teaches is that—any thought or way that is not wholly God's is altogether wrong and must be avoided."[70]

Here are some examples:

1. Garden of Eden—two trees, one allowed, one forbidden with a destiny of every human being hanging in the balance (Genesis 3).

2. Mt. Gerizim (of blessing) and Mt. Ebal (of cursing) The former promised the blessing of God on godliness; the latter declared the curse of God on wickedness (Deuteronomy 11:29).

3. Jesus spoke of the "narrow road," and the "wide road" (Matthew 7:13).

4. There are those who are "with" us and "against" us (2 Kings 6:16; Mark 9:40).

5. All through the Bible, one can observe dichotomies of life and death, truth and falsehood, good and evil, light and darkness, Kingdom of God and kingdom of Satan (Ecclesiastes 3).–"for everything there is a season: a time to be born, and a time to die; a time to weep and a time to laugh; a time to kill and a time to heal."[71]

In other words, we must be able to distinguish the ways of God from all other ways. Elijah on Mt. Carmel told the prophets of Baal to "choose this day who you will serve." Whether we realize it or not, we are all going to have to choose every day of our lives because sadly, today's religious teaching is a mixture of liberalism, political correctness, unorthodox ideas, vain philosophies, and cultic notions mixed together with God's truth in an unholy amalgam.

We need the antidote to the poison water around us as God gave Moses at Marah. The antidote is the unencumbered Word of God.

I am thinking of those who have gone before us who chose and faced persecution. It was good enough for Polycarp, who was burned at the stake February 1, 185 A.D., after having been encouraged to deny his Lord. He told the crowd, "Eighty-six years have I served him, and He has done me no wrong: how can I blaspheme my Savior and King?"[72]

It was good enough for Martin Luther 1,400 years later. "When pressed to defend his 95 Theses at a debate arranged by the Catholic hierarchy in June of 1519 in the city of Leipzig, he actually denied the ultimate authority of the church (and of church councils) in favor of the authority of scripture, a stance that evoked gasps of dismay from the faithful Catholics and sharpened the gulf between the Wittenberg friar and his church."[73] (And made him a fugitive for the rest of his life).

And it will be good enough for us who are appointed to live in the last days of this present world system, confronting the possibility that our heads could be chopped off for the truth as well. If after being challenged by the average theologue to be more "open-minded", you might retort, "Open minds are like open windows. You have to put in screens to keep out the bugs."

KING SOLOMON

Walking away from continuum thinking and developing an antithetical mindset was not only important for the priesthood, it also was important for kingship (1 Kings 3:3–14). In this group of Scriptures, the Lord appeared to Solomon while at Gibeon in a dream by night. God said, "Ask what I shall give you." It reminds me of the iconic genie in a bottle. Make your wish. Just think of it, Solomon could have asked for anything he wanted. It seemed to be open-ended.

Solomon wisely asked for an "understanding mind," that "I may discern between good and evil." The Hebrew word for to "judge between" means "interval or space between" so as to "separate things from one another at their points of difference in order to distinguish them."[74] An example would be a basket of apples or oranges. It then becomes a process of knowing God's thoughts and ways through separating those things that differ. Voila! Discernment!

Jewelers use this method with respect to precious stones.

Bankers use this method with respect to counterfeit money.

Jesus did this in Matthew 16:2–3 to discern the weather patterns according to the color of the sky. Through a process of discrimination, a person can make judgments and decisions. Paul did this in 1 Corinthians 11:29 to exhort the saints as to discerning the Lord's body in communion.

Still, during the feast of Tabernacles, Jesus told the Jews, "If on the Sabbath a man receives circumcision, so that the Law of Moses may not be broken, are you angry with me because on the Sabbath I made a man's body whole well? Do not judge by appearances, but judge with right judgment" (John 7:23–24).

The upshot is we have the ability to ascertain the mind of God (1 Corinthians 2:12–13)

BRINGING IT HOME

Today, television and the media clearly have the upper hand in molding our hearts and minds. In Steven Garofalo's recent book

Right for You but Not for Me, he says, "The greatest singular influence in molding, training, and impacting the minds and hearts of younger generations and the general population is Mass Media."

More homes have televisions than have indoor plumbing. The average home has television on six hours and seventeen minutes a day. The average American teenager watches nearly three hours of television daily. The average American child will watch 5,000 hours of television before first grade and 19,000 hours by high school graduation. The lifetime total for television viewing is nine years by age sixty-five.[75]

Continuing, Garofalo says, "When you consider political correctness and the media—through news, television programing and movies–have they not become the judge and jury of all things moral? Many liberal media professionals work hard to inject moral relativism into culture's DNA."[76]

The society is becoming increasingly morally thinned out with each passing generation. We are losing ground. I believe we would all do well to be reminded of the parable of the talents (Matthew 25:14–30). We have been given one life, specific gifts, a finite amount of time, and opportunities to use the *talents* that God has given us to fulfill His mission.

Alister McGrath asks the question in a recent book *Mere Discipleship*, "So, how can the churches be both culturally relevant (contextualized) and at the same time counter cultural (gospel centered)? How can it be distinct from its context, yet remain connected to or embedded within it?"[77] And furthermore, "How can the church remain firmly in the public square rather than in some isolated ghetto with its own private language and habits of thought that many of our contemporaries, whether with affection or derision, see as quaint relics of a discarded past?"[78]

We must become "imaginatively compelling" in order to attract others to this pilgrim community of faith as we pass through this world. I believe the Holy Spirit is the key—one ear to heaven and one ear in the community, discerning every step of the way.

LOGOS VS. RHEMA

A number of years ago, some distinction between two important New Testament words impacted our discussion on discernment. Those words are logos and rhema both of which mean "Word."

Logos is seen in the familiar verse of John 1:1: "In the beginning was the word, and the word was with God and the word was God." This Word was essentially the incarnate mind of God— the intention of God expressing God's total creative will and message to mankind. Jesus is, in fact, the logos of God. Think of it this way—a word is always an expression of a thought. Jesus is the perfect expression of God's thought to man. It's not only God's word to us but God's deed to us. It involves the Holy acts of God in our world.

Rhema, on the other hand, means the spoken word of God, regardless of who is doing the speaking. Rhema does not refer to the written word, which distinguishes it from logos. One can observe this in John 17:8: "for I have given them thy words which thou gavest me …" (RSV). Or consider Acts 5:20; "Go and stand in the temple and speak to the people all the words of life" (RSV).

Rhema is about hearing and obeying. It is not mere information, but a dynamic event. It is the word that changes people's lives, giving the Church its sense of direction.[79] So the *Rhema* word can be a personal word to an individual, a group, or a church.[80] Here is where the rub comes in:

In the early Charismatic renewal, distinctions were being made between logos and rhema. Many people of a prophetic bent were saying that the rhema word was more powerful and direct on which to focus our intention and actions of our Christian witness. This could come to us in a personal prophetic word or a dynamic thought process in our pious attempt to connect with God, such as a verse or Scripture jumping off the page of a book we're reading.

One leader wrote: "Unity is not built on a relationship to my brother, but on a response to the word of God. Thus you may have as much unity as you have agreement on the *Rhema* of the Spirit."[81] The problem here is if there is no agreement in terms of the rhema of the Spirit, then it becomes impossible to maintain any working fellowship. As a result, separation from other Christians may be necessary.[82]

One can see that division on the above basis would be never-ending, resulting in mindless division for no real reason. Two basic concepts counter this kind of thinking. First, there is no clear distinction between logos and rhema in the Scriptures. At the core level, they remain the Word of God. The only difference is in the presentation mode, not in the core of the word. Similar to saying there is a difference in the presentation mode of God the Father to God the Son or between God the Son to God the Spirit. They still remain one even though their presentation impacts us somewhat differently.

To lift rhema (a prophetic spoken word) above the written word is a false dichotomy. Secondly, Christian unity is always based on our relationship to Christ through salvation. If we are born again, we are connected...period. We don't create unity; we maintain it. It is automatic by virtue of our relationship to the Savior (Ephesians 2:16; 4:3). If any brother of sister is "in Christ," they are connected to one another, regardless to their individual response to logos or rhema.[83]

Finally, because we need to hear from the Lord on various aspects of our journey, which may not have chapter and verse, both logos and rhema work together to complete a unified witness in our experience. Only then can a person realize complete confidence in the process of discernment and Christian living. *Selah!*

CHAPTER 4

A PROPHETIC CHURCH

GOD HAS GIVEN US THE PROPHETIC AS A WAY to awaken a sense of His intentions to motivate godliness in the affairs of man. Hearing His voice can be an extremely stimulating experience. The confidence to know God is actually speaking to us through the prophetic does wonders for affirming who He made us to be. Furthermore, the prophetic is the next step in the discernment process.

> Connect with god first and allow your discernment to be the door for spiritual revelation that goes beyond your thoughts, feelings, opinions, or faith. God wants you to take what you discern and talk to him about it. Then he can reveal his deep heart and share his thoughts about it.[84]

I love what Shawn Bolz says about the purpose of the prophetic: "Prophetic ministry is about your being a gateway in God's thoughts, emotions, and heart for others through a connection to

Him.[85] The goal is love, rather than information."[86] "By doing this, we see what God sees, hear what God hears, and speak what God speaks so we can all live the way God loves. Revelation is given to us so we can carry a piece of God's heart from eternity into this world."[87] Solomon reminded us after all, "... also he has put eternity into man's mind ..." (Ecclesiastes 3:11).

Since the prophetic was only recently reintroduced into the life of the Church (1980s–1990s), it will help to just lay down some ground rules in the beginning. The Charismatic renewal was the womb of the prophetic movement, and I entered it during the heart of the movement (1969–1970).

Since that period of time, I have been privileged to be a part of this ongoing stream for many years, both meeting and ministering with some of the profound "prophetic stars" of the movement. In addition, being a pastor for thirty-eight years and a leader in a citywide network of leaders, I speak from personal experience in the prophetic.

THE WIDE-ANGLE VIEW

When we speak of the prophetic in the broadest sense of the word, we mean any supernatural knowledge given to men by God. The prophetic at this point becomes an umbrella term to include more than the gift of prophecy (foretelling and forthtelling); it also includes visions, dreams, visitations, trances, perceptions, words of knowledge and wisdom, and other gifts.[88] Shawn Bolz calls it "the ability to know what is available or what is in the heart of God for the future. It is knowing what God wants to do or what he is developing someone or something to do."[89]

So friends, what we are talking about is simply hearing the voice of God in our lives. In fact, there is no greater joy, nothing that will deliver more pleasure than walking in partnership with God. It grieves me to think that much of the Church has been taught that prophesy is a first-century mystery, so that a "grown-up" church has moved beyond such experience.

Kim Clement, one of the great prophetic voices of our day, said in his book on the prophetic when asked by Larry King what the difference was between a psychic and a prophet, "Psychics speak to the dead who are 'living'; prophets speak to the living who are 'dead.'" Then he went on to clarify: "Some people are walking and breathing in this world but in actual fact are spiritually dead. You only have one life to live on this earth—why should you have to wait until you have died before you can be reached?"[90]

So here is the good news—we are all prophetic. Think about it.

No one can ever become a Christian without receiving a direct, personal revelation from the Holy Spirit. Jesus explains, "No one can come to me unless the Father who sent me draws him, and I will raise him up at the last day." No one is saved without some sense of "hearing from God." So if you are a Christian, you have already entered the prophetic realm (John 5:25; 6:44–45).[91]

The prophetic, of course, has always been a part of the history of God's people on the earth. Let us consider an example from the history from the Methodist movement birthed in England. Theologian John Fletcher was the most influential person in Methodism next to John and Charles Wesley. In 1777, he arrived near death at the conference for Methodist preachers held at Bristol, England.

John Wesley knelt at his side, and all the preachers joined him. Wesley prayed for Fletcher's restoration to health and a longer ministerial career. Mr. Wesley closed his prayer with this prophecy: "He shall not die, but live, and declare the works of the Lord." Mr. Fletcher did recover and lived another eight years.[92]

The chapter on the prophetic in one of my previous books lays it out nicely: "The import of the prophetic involves three things all chained together: listening, understanding, and obeying. Psalm 19:14 should be a silent prayer upon our lips at all times: 'Let the words of my mouth and the meditation of my heart be acceptable in thy sight, O Lord, my rock and my redeemer.'"[93]

You may say, "I don't feel worthy." Well, join the crowd! Remember, it is not about us. It is about God and His call over our lives. For instance:

- Moses said: "O Lord, I am not eloquent, either heretofore or since thou hast spoken to thy servant; but I am slow of speech and of tongue" (Exodus 4:10 RSV).

- Isaiah said: "Woe is me for! For I am lost: for I am a man of unclean lips …" (Isaiah 6:5 RSV).

- Jeremiah said, "Ah, Lord God! Behold, I do not know how to speak, for I am only a youth. … But you, gird up your loins; arise, and say to them everything that I command you …" (Jeremiah 1:6, 17 RSV).

THE PROPHETIC AND VISION

Just begin to sense what God wants, and then be bold enough to speak it forth. Similar to almost everything else in our Christian walk, it boils down to an act of obedience.[94] This is very closely akin to what the Apostle Paul speaks about in Ephesians 1:17–21, especially verses 18–19: "having the eyes of your hearts enlightened, that you may know what is the hope to which he has called you, what are the riches of his glorious inheritance in the saints, and what is the immeasurable greatness of his power in us who believe ..." (RSV).

Every born-again believer has two sets of eyes—the physical eyes and the eyes of our hearts. It will help us to pause here for a moment and really let this truth sink in.

This letter by the Apostle Paul was what was known as a circular letter believed to have been given to multiple churches such as Laodicea (Colossians 4:13), Hierapolis (Colossians 4:13), Troas (Acts 20:5), Colossae (Colossians 1:2) and Ephesus. As we look at this curious phrase, "the eyes of your heart," we find that this is the only place in the Bible where this phrase occurs.

However, the expression is found in Classical Greek literature. In means: "the seat of all human life" (not the organ that pumps blood); it is the center of consciousness; it is the place of understanding; it is the seat of the will; it is the place where human emotions are sensed and out of which they are expressed. In other words, it is the center of the whole human personality.

So Paul is praying that the eyes of our hearts may be enlightened. He understands something that isn't clear to everybody. He understands that you can see with your eyes and not really see, that you can hear with your ears and not really hear. So he prays that the eyes of their hearts would be enlightened.[95]

"Another way to say it is that the spirit of revelation is basically God's Spirit keeping us connected to his thoughts and heart for us and his Son. It's when the person and nature of God manifests to our understanding, spirit, and emotions.[96] This will prove to be a vital connection in the days ahead as we confront a wayward and sullen cultural America."

One of the names for the prophetic office in the Old Testament is seer. The Hebrew word is *ra'ah* and literally means to see as in a vision. It is used by Samuel in 1 Chronicles 29:29. Other meanings include "to gaze"; "to look upon"; and to "perceive."[97] This individual is receiving the word in a visual way and is trying to figure it out enough on the spot to verbalize what it is exactly they are seeing. Many times, they will wait until they feel the anointing to release the God-view to others.

Timing is important. The emphasis is on the prophet's revelatory relationship with God. This person actually sees before they hear. Then the two are linked together in a vision that is spoken and made relevant to a situation at hand.

One can read this process in Revelation 1:10, 12 with the Apostle John: "I was in the Spirit on the Lord's Day, and I heard behind me a loud voice like the sound of a trumpet ... Then I turned to see the voice that was speaking with me ..." Is it not interesting that John turned to "see" the voice, not "hear" the voice?

Kim Clement calls this "optical fusion"; "the combining of images from two eyes to form a single visual percept. There are two sights that must be combined, God's sight and your sight. And the beautiful thing about optical fusion is that God needs your sight."[98]

I find this fascinating, though I have experienced it on several occasions in my life, including right before I left for a conference where I was scheduled to speak in Kansas City a few years ago:

> I did have a significant dream the day before I left for the Kairos conference at IHOP in Kansas City (October 2017) The conference was a celebration of the forty-year anniversary of the 1977 Conference on the Charismatic Renewal in the Christian churches.

Here was my dream: I arrived and proceeded directly to a reception gathering for the leaders of the conference. After a brief time, one of the organizers took me directly to the venue where I began to weep the closer we got to the building. By the time we got in the building, I could not speak and was overcome with the Spirit of God. There was a huge image of the Ark of the Covenant on the wall (projection), and the man said they had the real Ark there and were going to unveil it to the conference.

I sat down in the front row with another leader (Gordon Robertson from CBN), who was already at our conference. They brought the ARK out, and the entire room was so overcome, no one could speak or even stand. The thing that struck me was that there were no cell phone pictures going off. Amazing!

The ARK, of course, contained three items: part of the stone tablets from Sinai; manna from heaven; and Aaron's rod which budded. God said that He was going to establish those three things during our conference. The tablets were the Word of God, Aaron's rod was the power of God, and the manna was the life of God, all of which would be on display at our conference with great unity and respect for His coming at the end of the age.

We, in part, were forerunners, signaling to the larger Body of Christ that unity and the power of the Spirit (John 17:20–23) as we approach the last great ingathering and the coming of the end of the age. As I left the building to go back to the other building where we would stay the night, I looked west. Two parallel tornados were on the outskirts of the city. I went into the building (not afraid) and took shelter in the basement. End of dream.

I did share this vision with the conference, which significantly helped confirm what the Lord was trying to accomplish in the event.

KEYING IN ON THE CORE

It will be of great value to remember the overall purpose of the prophetic which is enumerated for us by the Apostle Paul in 1 Corinthians 14:1: "Make love your aim, and earnestly desire the spiritual gifts, especially that you may prophesy" (RSV). And what does this release in the speaker and produce in the hearer? "Edification, exhortation, and comfort" (verse 3). Let's take a closer look.

First, **edification[upbuilding]**—*oikodomen.* This is the same root word as for "edifice" or "building." It means to build up, construct, confirm, establish, and improve. When the Jews referred to the building of the temple in John 2:20, they used this word. Peter used it referring to believers "being built into a spiritual house" (1Peter 2:5 RSV). Paul instructs us to "keep encouraging one another so that none of you is hardened by the lure of sin (Hebrew 3:13 RSV). In 1 Thessalonians 5:11, we are to "… encourage one another and build each other up, just as in fact you are doing" (RSV). This remains a powerful relevant gift to the Church in a world where there is so much darkness and people without hope. David, Saul, Timothy, and Jesus were the recipients of this prophetic gift. The stewardship of our words almost demands that we give prime attention to encouragement.

Second, **exhortation (urge on)**—*paraklesin*. The meaning is to root for someone in a race or a competition. Webster defines it as "urge or incite by strong argument, advice or appeal; to admonish earnestly." Strong's Concordance explains it as "an act of crying out, wooing, or calling near." We are talking about prompting the Church to draw near to God. True prophets will discern God's intention for His people and then cautiously urge them on into that thing. We are not talking about harsh ultimatums or portraying God as angry or unmerciful. Excessive pressure is not a part of biblical protocol. We are talking about such things as exhorting the weary and encouraging the discouraged not to give up.

Finally, **consolation [comfort]**—*paramuthian.* This means a calling alongside to strengthen. It denotes physical, mental, and spiritual refreshment. Jesus was commissioned to "comfort those who mourn in Zion." 11Corinthians 1, tells us that our God is a God of all comfort. In 1 Thessalonians 5, we are told to "comfort those who are cast down" (RSV).

Remember "… mercy triumphs over judgment" (James 2:13 RSV).

I urge the Church to excel in these gifts. We would do well to keep these three overall directives in view as we release the prophetic in our neighborhood of influence.

THE PROPHETIC AND THE FUTURE

There is a certain flow that the prophetic will assume as we approach the end of God's timetable on Earth. I believe that it has been given to us to ready those and ourselves around us for the consummation of the ages. Perhaps we are the generation to welcome the coming of the Lord. If not, then we are certainly the ones to announce it. Many are realizing the earth has begun a time of transitional labor that will bring to birth the fullness of the Kingdom of God and the end of the age. Be mindful that the Kingdom of God is really here, but not fully here.

Consequently, into this mix of salvation and judgment, the Church will be called to live as a prophetic witness. It will be an accelerated heightened and deepened witness to Christ than has been seen previously. There will be revival and refreshing as well as judgment preceding the end (Acts 3:19–21). If we are approaching the end of time, then we the Church have work to do.

Read what Michael Sullivant writes in his book *Prophetic Etiquette*, "The churches corporate strength and power is not in military, economic or political might—carnal weapons. Her authority is spiritual and moral as she functions like a conscience among the nations. Her presence in the earth provides moral 'salt and light'— preserving influence and truth—holding back both the full range of Satan and the just wrath of God."[99]

One more thing to consider as we move toward God's prophetic timetable. We live in a day of prophetic preparation for the coming of the Lord. Some have identified the Church's witness in these days as a forerunner spirit. This is a biblical theme where "prophetic heralds" were sent ahead of the Lord to announce the coming visitation of the King to the people. This was literally the method used in ancient culture (2 Chronicles 30:5–6). Also note Elijah in 1 Kings 18:46. Can we conceive of this in an atmosphere of love for the lost?

The Apostle Paul reminds us of the proper direction to move forward (1 Corinthians 13: 11). If we are moving in the right direction, we are moving toward a maturing posture. We must be able to tolerate the uncertainties of life—with deep trust in God. This is a process.

Isaiah 28:10 says, "… precept upon precept, line upon line …." Everything around us in the natural world matures, so why shouldn't we? It is unnatural for baby Christians to remain in the baby stage. It's antithetical to the purpose of God. We are going to do it by sinking our roots deep into the soil of the Kingdom and by a determined regimen of intimacy with God. God will settle for nothing less than the full attention of twenty-first century Christians, especially if we are to address the consequences of the '60s inheritance with effective prophetic wisdom and insight.

CONCLUDING THOUGHTS

Is it just me, because it seems like the Church is always trying to play catchup to the cultural surroundings in which it finds itself.

Perhaps it is because the Church has been focused on naval gazing rather than star gazing. The Apostle Peter tells us straight up, "And we have the prophetic word made more sure. You will do well to pay attention to this as to a lamp shining in a dark place, until the day dawns and the morning star rises in your hearts" (2 Peter 1:19). Jesus is our star, so if we are going to gaze anywhere, it ought to be on Jesus, not on a set of doctrines, however important doctrines may be.

The Church for too much of its history has been creed-centered. A creed is a mental ascent to a "right-believing" sequence approved by the hierarchy of the Church. The word "creed" comes from the Latin word *credere*—"to believe."

The history of the Church is a history of conflict over who was right in their opinion (or creed). Over time, this intellectualizing of Christianity shaped future generations of Protestants especially where right belief replaced biblically defined faith (hearing God through the Spirit and obeying).[100]

In essence, we don't really believe God; we only believe our beliefs about God. A person may have all their ducks in a row, not realizing they are "sitting ducks" to be picked off (ignored) by the waiting world.

One can see this clearly played out in the '60s "while the church was measuring the length of skirts and the length of hair, scientists were discovering a greater means of transport; Bill Gates was gazing into the mystical ball of Microsoft, and women were legislating abortion, removing the rights of the unborn."[101]

In his book *Call Me Crazy but I'm Hearing God*, Kim Clement argues, "the short skirts did lengthen, but it did not stop the adultery; the long hair did shorten, but it did not stop the rebellion; and millions of babies have died and billions of dollars have supplied the wrong people with power."[102] All this while the Church was still naval gazing. God help us to see the truth.

As we bring this chapter on the prophetic to a close, let us muse on the purpose of the prophetic in the first place. Dr. Jon Ruthven, my mentor for my doctoral program, had put it quite succinctly. He said, "The difference between the message of the Bible and the message of traditional (human) religion is the emphasis on two different kinds of knowing: the biblical "knowing," that is, the experience of God, vs. merely knowing information about God."[103] He goes on to say, "The message and goal the Bible emphasizes, then, is the process of the Spirit of God revealing God's will (instruction, wisdom) directly into believers' hearts. This will then enable believers to achieve the ultimate goal of intimacy with God himself and his glory."[104]

This alone will empower us to confront a waiting world. So what are we waiting for? Finish the book, and get started.

CHAPTER 5

UNDERSTANDING THE FEAR OF THE LORD

IN ORDER TO UNDERSTAND THE UNIQUE CALLING of God's people in history and link that calling to the fear of the Lord, we must begin with a review of ancient Israel. This topic is extremely important not only for a historical base, but also for grounding in the authority which God has granted to His people as they approach the end of history.

The fear of the Lord is a concept widely neglected in the modern-day Church, yet it's crucial as the Church approaches extreme days in the not-too-distant future. A pressure (tribulation) is coming upon the world like history has never seen before and without being grounded in this concept, the Church will fold.

However, we have the sure Word of God that a strong remnant of God's people will stand strong and prevail during the oncoming pressure cooker of persecution and tribulation. We have it on good authority that "... The kingdom of the world has become the kingdom of our Lord and of his Christ, and he shall reign for ever and ever."[105] This will take place because "... they have conquered him by the blood of the lamb and the word of their testimony ....”[106]

THE MYSTERY OF ANCIENT ISRAEL

The Old Testament (OT) world was a Hellenistic Syrian world that was religiously dominated with icons, idols, and images of various gods. The idols were a kind of mediator of spirituality between the people and the god that the image represented. The Egyptians had Osiris, the sun god. The Canaanites had Baal, the fertility god. The Greeks had Zeus, the patriarch god of their pantheon. And so on and so forth.

Into this mix, God summoned a nation called Israel. The one stark reality that distinguished Israel from all the other ancient people was the absence of any images in any of their worship. Furthermore, with these images of the heathen peoples, the deity, could reveal itself in trees, in animals, and in stars. The image was the medium between god and man; it was the bearer of revelation.

But with Israel, the revelation comes directly from the presence of the living God, who claims to be the only God with no rivals. In the Ten Commandments, God reveals that the worship of images is lumped together with murder, adultery, and idolatry. Pretty heavy stuff.

So here came God right out of the gate, in one fell swoop, rendering Israel unique, and I mean unique, with this heart-to-heart on Mt. Sinai. (See Exodus 20:3–4).

Why is this so important to God? Because He knows that man is innately religious, and he will have a god! He, of course, wants him to have the right God.

You see Israel is a nation commandeered by God and called forth by revelation beginning with Abraham and continuing with

Moses some 400 years later. Their ability to elude the grip of this God proved futile. They were His people, and He was their God. Just like your parents were your parents, and that is the end of it.

And Israel, you must know early on that images and idols are a waste of time when you can hear directly from the God of heaven. It is the first order of business for Israel (Psalm 28:1). When God is silent, man is undone and fears death. (Deuteronomy 32:47, 8:3). When God is silent, hunger arises (Amos 8:11). Since they are going to maintain this ongoing relationship until the end of the world, this conversation with God, sometimes refusing, sometimes wondering, but never cut loose. The Lord God wants her primal calling to remain intact. They were a people of one God, unique in the ancient world.

There were times when the sheer wonder of it continued to amaze Israel.[107]

HEARING GOD SPEAK

When Israel heard this God speak, it was not a philosophical platform; it was a historical event, from a thundering prophet, or an earthquake at the right time, or a miraculous deliverance from a foreign power, or a tablet of stone—something we can track in space and time. It was history, something we even today can look back on (for example, the Exodus, the conquest, and the fall of northern and southern kingdoms.)

God's words involved instructions, consolations, and disclosures of divine plans (Psalm 103:7, Amos 3:7). So they invaded history and became its motor, especially the prophet's word, giving Israel her forward movement and her goals. How else could Abraham leave a perfectly good life in another country and traipse across the ancient East from Iraq to Jerusalem with nothing but a word (voice of God)? Amazingly, he received his commission through the prophetic, and he was off to the races. I keep emphasizing this because if we are to understand our calling in history, especially end-times history, it is important to know the dynamic of this conversation between God and Israel. I can tell you, it finds no counterpart in the history of religions. It is unique.

As Gerhard Von Rad, a noted Old Testament scholar from a previous generation says, "It begins with God and says that man can only be understood at all if one begins with God, and every other form of understanding can lead only to distortions and diminutions. God took His pattern, His model for the upper chambers, the divine world when He created man, and man can be understood only from above."[108] I might add, this becomes our ace in the hole, called and commissioned by Jesus Christ to speak to the times we are living in with the authority of heaven and our mystery as well.[109]

This is the mystery of ancient Israel. We don't have to remake the world in our image. We can see it as God sees it even today. We too with Job can utter this refrain: "Indeed these are the mere edges of His ways, and how small a whisper we hear of Him!" In Job 26:14, Job makes an observation: "… But the thunder of His power who can understand?" (NKJV). Everything else is a nothing. It is either God or nothingness (the folly of idols).[110]

So in light of this reality, thank you very much, but I will not be getting up at 3 a.m. so I can be at Walmart at 4 a.m. to worship at your altar of commercial Christmas on Black Friday. I have more urgent business at hand. The world is going to hell in a hand basket while many go their merry way preoccupied with Netflixs. It's time to sound the alarm, and this book is part of that alarm.

When Israel decided that day at Shechem to cling to this God alone, God took them seriously. How do I know that? Joshua renewed the covenant with the God of ancient Israel, and God gets real focused at covenant time.[111]

Each generation of Israel had to re-up as far as the First Commandment was concerned. It became a kind of daily religious guerrilla war. They were constantly in the midst of a cultic world where little gods were nipping at their heels.

All of this becomes curiously reminiscent of the Church in America. Did they need the fertility gods for the blessings on their crops? Did they need the medicine gods for the healing of illness and disease? Were they going to be defeated when the Assyrian king sent armies into Palestine? The answer was no!

By the way, we fight the same wars. Our idols today are not so much little wooden carvings, but instead political correctness, homosexual marriage, insider trading, greed in lending, sexual infidelity, educational attainment, wealth and prosperity, position and power, political ideology, Democrat/Republican. We have our idols, or should I say they have us. But we also have revelation for the Most High God. Which one are we going to follow?

THE FEAR OF THE LORD

The fear of God was made unmistakable in the First Commandment—"You shall have no other gods before me." However, it seems the inertia of history has caused a slowdown, creating a drag on this most important concept. Without the fear of God, the people of God cannot withstand the times in which we are living. We will most assuredly fold. So let's go a bit deeper into the fear of the Lord and see where it takes us.

What exactly is the fear of the Lord? It means more than "reverential trust." It includes this and yet is much more. King Solomon, following a life of comfort and wisdom, comes close to a definition when he makes this final statement in Ecclesiastes 12:13-14: "The end of the matter; all has been heard. Fear God, and keep his commandments; for this is the whole duty of man. For God will bring every deed into judgment, with every secret thing, whether good or evil."[112]

Sounds rather straightforward to me. Here is a working definition I received years ago at a Bill Gothard ministers' conference on basic youth conflicts: "The continual awareness that I am in the presence of a holy, just, and Almighty God, and that every thought, word, action, and deed is open before him, and is being judged by him." [113]

God has created us for his pleasure and intimate friendship. If we have the fear of the Lord upon us, we will want to please our Creator because we will be continually aware of His presence.

Think of it; in light of the previous chapter on the prophetic, we are on speaking terms with God. What Moses experienced as a privileged calling, we all can experience as a day-to-day communication with our Creator. How awesome is that?

First of all, Jesus warns, "For nothing is hid that shall not be made manifest, nor anything secret that shall not be known and come to light."[114] Adding to this, He continues, "Therefore whatever you have said in the dark shall be heard in the light, and what you have whispered in private rooms shall be proclaimed upon the housetops."[115] It's time the Church begins with earnest to walk in this awareness. Even the psalmist knew this a thousand years before Jesus. He asks, "He who planted the ear, does he not hear? He who formed the eye, does he not see?[116]

David's son, Solomon wrote, "For a man's ways are before the eyes of the Lord, and he watches all his paths."[117]

Remember the all-seeing eye of Sauron in J. R. R. Tolkien's trilogy *The Lord of the Rings*? Well, it is kind of like that only in a good way.

On the other hand, what if all our thoughts, words, and deeds were projected on a big screen for all to see? That might be a problem because most of us would not like others to have a front-row seat during that showing. We all would be embarrassed. It is called the "fear of man," which becomes a deterrent to walking in the fear of the Lord. We could even define the fear of man as being more concerned about man's reaction to our actions than God's reaction to our actions. One could call it "caving in to peer pressure." "wanting to impress someone else," and "wanting to look good in the eyes of others." In biblical terms, this would be labeled a "snare."

A snare is a device that incorporates a noose for a small animal or prey. You see, we can get "trapped" when we are snared by the fear of man. At times, one can actually feel the snare go around you—you become afraid of what someone else is going to think.

There are actually many different kinds of snares in the Bible. Some examples are false gods, sinful covenants, silver and gold, evil associations, idolatry, broken vows, friendships with violent men, greed, and evil caught unawares. Can you think of a time when you might have been trapped by a snare? One way to avoid its grip is to learn to communicate with the Lord as you go through your day. Tell God what is on your heart, and He will tell you what is on His heart. Be willing to act on what the Lord instructs.

I have observed over the years that pastors are particularly vulnerable to the fear of man. The Church is full of well-meaning people who will try to overly influence you over this or that issue. We back down from confrontation so as to not breach a friendship, and there we are, caught in the snare.

During an administrative board meeting on one occasion, I was confronted by the chairman (a life-long Democrat). He challenged me not to refer to the president (currently Jimmy Carter) from the pulpit in a disparaging way.

In an interview with *Playboy* magazine, President Carter made the statement that "looking upon a woman with lust was not the same as actually committing adultery."

I mentioned it in a sermon, showing how the Scripture says just the opposite, and Carter was wrong. I told him during the meeting, "Don't ever tell me what to say or not say from the pulpit! It is sovereign territory, and I will speak what the Lord tells me."[118]

Things got a bit heated until another well-respected brother jumped in and urged us onto other business. You see, even if you make mistakes, and we all do, God will honor the spirit of your life that desires to honor Him.

Jesus, of course, is our prototype. He never shrunk back from confrontation because He had "... the spirit of ... the fear of the Lord" upon His life (Isaiah 11:2). He says in John 5:19, "... Truly, truly, I say to you, the Son can so nothing of his own accord, but only what he sees the Father doing; for whatever he does, that the Son does likewise" (RSV). This is precisely why He only healed one man at the pool of Bethesda because He only saw God touching one man.

He also cut through all the haze when speaking to the Pharisees, declaring, "... before Abraham was, I AM!" (John 8:58). He called the Pharisees a "a brood of vipers" (Matthew 12:34); and likened them to "white-washed tombs ... full of dead man's bones (Matthew 23:27)." Talk about confrontation.

In John 7, Jesus's disciples tried to push Him to go to Jerusalem during the Feast of Tabernacles and "show yourself to the world."

But He responds in John 7:8, "I am not going up to this feast, for my time has not yet fully come." He remained in Galilee, not being pushed in a direction the Father had not authorized. Sometimes it's all about timing.

DIGGING DEEPER

There are several Hebrew words in the Old Testament translated FEAR. The Hebrew; "yirah" and "yare" translate to fear, dred, terror, timidity, dismay, and awe.[119] I like the word "awe" because it captures something beyond for our experience.

The fear of the Lord is not being scared or frightened that God is going to punish us the minute we step out of line. Rather, it means a respect, a reverence for the master of the universe. There is simply not enough awe in the Church today.

In addition, the principle Greek words for fear are "phobos" and "phobeo" (Gr.) where we get our word phobia; an irrational fear or aversion to something.[120] These Greek words translate to such things as terror, alarm, reverence, respect, and fright depending on the context.

As one can see, some of the words are rather positive and some are negative. The point is there is a mystery in divine holiness which produces in man a sense of terror. For example, we see Jacob at Bethel encountering God in a dream. "Then Jacob awoke from his sleep and said, 'Surely the Lord is in this place; and I did not know it. And he was afraid, and said, How awesome is this place! This is none other than the house of God, and this is the gate of heaven.'"[121] Compare this with Moses's experience at Sinai or Isaiah's experience in the temple in Isaiah 6. These encounters to the manifestation of God resulted in blind terror and trembling, accompanied by a perception of God's glory and great concern and love for man.

Each one walked away with a tangible new history— Moses knowing God's name and purpose for Israel; Jacob with a promise of land and prosperity; and Isaiah with a promise to be sent as God's personal emissary to the nations.

From these and other stories in the Old Testament, one can deduce that the people of God were enjoined to love God absolutely and exclusively. In fact, the devout Jew was to recite a mantra several times a day reminding them of this exclusive relationship. It was called the Shema: "Hear, O Israel: the Lord our God is one Lord, and you shall love the Lord your God with all your heart, and with all your soul, and with all your might."[122]

The Hebrew finds himself in a context with fearful dimensions. It is this exacting and inclusive sense of absolute love, that the fear of the Lord became the principle of human behavior and the beginning of wisdom.[123] Any thought of evil, rebellion, or compromise creates in the follower of God a sense of anguish.

Therefore, the term the "fear of the Lord" (yir'ah/Yahweh) is an umbrella term describing the entire religion and experience of the ancient Hebrew faith and transported into the New Testament with the birth of Jesus Christ (John 1:1–14). It is a comprehensive term directly linked to one's encounter with the absolute majesty of a Holy God.

The popular Christian musician Steve Green sings it in the lyrics of his hit song "God and God Alone": "We shall never tire, of our one desire; God and God alone." It is the basis upon which our respect for God is maintained. It's not His accomplishments or strength of personality that commands our supreme devotion, but the righteousness of His character—and that is unchanging.

Listen to what the prophet Malachi says of Him as he closes the Old Testament:

> Then those who feared the Lord spoke with one another; the Lord heeded and heard them, and a book of remembrance was written before him of those who feared the Lord and thought on his name. "They shall be mine," says the Lord of hosts, "my special possession on the day when I act, and I will spare them as a man spares his son who serves him. Then once more you shall distinguish between the righteous and the wicked, between one who serves God and one who does not serve him."[124]

THE ECLIPSE OF ETHICS AND MORALITY IN TODAY'S WORLD

Solomon's famous words from the book of Ecclesiastes set the stage for our final thoughts in this chapter. He comments, "History merely repeats itself. It has all been done before. Nothing under the sun is truly new."[125]

The Church has failed to successfully navigate our present world with any semblance of godliness while forfeiting a credible witness to a world lost in sin and corruption. We are aware of the concept of the fear of the Lord but have settled for so much less. We have definitely lost the battle of the culture wars and are well into retreat. Sadly, history has repeated itself again. If we hold up the book of Judges as a mirror, we will see our reflection.

A brief review will set the stage. After Moses finished his forty-year trek into the wilderness with the children of Israel, Joshua his protégé, prepared to take the nation into the Promised Land. The first conquest was the city of Jericho, a story that is taught in every Sunday school in America at some point. It took about fifty years of conquest before the Israelites "owned" the land of Palestine for their own. During this period of history, it was like guerilla warfare, city by city, province by province.

The most unfortunate thing happened following their siege of the indigenous people. Israel, little by little, began to lose their distinctiveness. In many cases, after settling in and dividing the land out to the Twelve Tribes, they found themselves intermarrying with the conquered women and adopting allegiance to their gods along with their distinctive God Yahweh. Their religion became a mixture, what modern-day missiologists call "syncretism." This, in turn, led to backsliding in their religion and being oppressed by the very people they had just conquered. Their apostasy led to oppression, and their oppression to renewal and repentance.

Finally, they were delivered by judges who God would raise up, and the entire sequence would start all over again. This pattern prevailed some fifteen different times over many decades, even centuries.

The well-known summation verse, actually the last verse of the book of Judges, is very telling. It not only describes their weak and confused religious mentality, it also describes our culture today, including many in the modern-day church.

Think deeply on this verse and look at your own culture at the same time: "In those days there was no king in Israel; every man did what was right in his own eyes."[126]

In fact, America is very much like David's son Solomon. We have incurred wealth, wisdom, and women in our journey in history. Our wealth is respected the world over, much like the wealth of Queen of Sheba who visited Solomon on one occasion and was transfixed by his wealth.

Our wisdom, indicative of high-tech Silicon Valley, leads the world in the Space Age— twenty-first century. Our "women," i.e., our fascination with sexual promiscuity and leading the world in the production of pornography, has followed Solomon's bent toward his 700 wives and the just-can't-get-enough mentality. Again, like Solomon says, "Nothing under the Sun is truly new."

God has given us boundaries and parameters within which to live. He has the right to do this because He is God. He told Adam and Eve in the Garden, "You may freely eat of every tree of the garden; but of the tree of the knowledge of good and evil you shall not eat, for in the day that you eat of it you shall die."[127] I don't believe it was a split decision. She looked at the tree, and the fruit was pleasing to the eye, and she was hungry. Why not?

However, Eve transgressed the boundaries and plunged mankind into an interminable world of darkness.

And again today, God is calling the Church to make a choice. Who is going to set the rules? We have to choose. Eve took the bait of Satan, but in doing so, did not become like God, but she acted like God and so becoming a god unto herself.

Every generation since has to make that choice. When there is no king in the land, we know where the decision will fall. God is King in our life, or we are king unto ourselves. There is no middle ground. The greatest challenge the Church faces today is to return to the fear of the Lord as a lifestyle. We will not have the moral authority to confront the great eclipse of ethics and morality in the twenty-first century without making God the King in our lives. After all, it is the Kingdom of God that Jesus came to inaugurate.

He proclaimed at the outset of His public ministry, "… The time is fulfilled, and the kingdom of God is at hand; repent, and believe in the gospel."[128]

We are simply too far down the road of human experience to think we can finagle our way out of the societal quagmire besetting us today. There is no way out. We are at Custer's Last Stand.

I am reminded of the last words of a poem Liam Neeson recites in the movie *The Gray:* "once more into the fray, into the last good fight I'll ever know. Live and die on this day, live and die on this day."

CHAPTER 6

THE GOVERNMENT OF GOD IN THE EARTH

IN THE COURSE OF HUMAN EVENTS, MANKIND has always had some kind of governing principle or organizing method to help with regulating the day-to-day affairs of his life. These have usually taken the form of a combination of external rules and internal codes. This has been the observable experience of mankind for the last 5,000 years.

In addition, this organizing matrix has usually come about through a combination of community consensus imposed from a domineering stronger element (for example, a king or dictator) or by design as in the formation of the United States.

In the Bible, laws and mores were not the result of community consensus. They were divinely given by the Creator. God alone makes the rules because God alone is the author of life.

The very first governmental structure in the Bible was the family. God created Adam and Eve[129] and assigned them duties (to till and keep the garden), while naming the animal life around them and governing their world by being fruitful and multiplying.[130] All of this took some measure of personal skill, which the Creator designed into His world. God created man in His image and likeness, so man could also function with creative prowess and the ability to manage his world.

According to J. I. Packer, the image of God in man (Imago Dei) is seen in four levels, all of which will be important for our subsequent discussion. First is "Man is a rational being, able to form concepts, think thoughts, carry through trains of reasoning, make and execute plans, live for goals, distinguish right from wrong and beautiful from ugly, and relate to other intelligent beings."[131]

Second is "God, the creator, made us sub-creators under him, able and needing to find fulfillment in the creativity of art, science, construction, technology, scholarship, and the bringing of order out of various sorts of chaos."[132]

Third, God made us as stewards (as in deputy managers) to have dominion over the world in which he inhabits. Man is to harness, develop, and use the resources of God's world so that a culture of humanity could enjoy the fruit of this labor.[133]

Finally, God who is good originally made man good in the sense of naturally and spontaneously righteous. This, in turn, would allow man to respond to God by doing what God loves and avoiding what God hates or forbids.[134]

Having acknowledged this background, the present chapter will cover three central areas of government germane to our thesis of theological violence and its antecedents. They are government over Israel; government over the United States of America; and government revealed by Jesus of Nazareth known as the Kingdom of God.

THE GOVERNMENT OF ISRAEL

After having been delivered from bondage in Egypt, the nation of Israel was led to a place called Mt. Sinai in the Sinai Desert between Egypt and the Promised Land. It is here the Lord God disclosed His covenant and love to the nation of Israel. God's rule over His people (those who choose to follow Him)[135], is disclosed in Exodus 20.[136] God's law given at Sinai is the "touchstone" not only for Israel, but for all humanity as we will see later.[137] The Ten Commandments were burned into two tables of stone, containing in a general form the vital principles of all modern legal science, judicial, national, and international.[138]

The Ten Commandments are known in Jewish history as the "Torah." "which means in the first place of teaching, a doctrine, and a decision given for a particular case. Collectively, the word means the whole body of rules governing men's relations with God and with each other."[139]

Inclusive in these five books are "God's instructions for his people, the prescriptions which his people had to observe in their moral, social, and religious life."[140]

Jesus Christ reduced these to two: "You shall love the Lord your God with all your heart, and with all your soul, and with all your mind. ... And a second is like it, You shall love your neighbor as yourself. On these two commandments depend all the law and the prophets."[141]

The name of the God who gave the Ten Commandments was and is "Yahweh" (YHWH). The name was disclosed to Moses at a place called the burning bush (Exodus 3). His name means "He who causes to be—what comes into existence," or "He who causes the Hosts (of Israel to come into existence.)"[142]

Furthermore, W.F. Albright, who was the "dean" of archeology in the twentieth century, makes this categorical statement: "It is absurd to deny that Moses was actually the founder of Israelite commonwealth and the framer of Israel's religious system. This fact is emphasized so unanimously by tradition that it may be regarded as absolutely certain."[143]

This brief history sets the parameters for the Nation of Israel and much of the Jewish people, even up to the present day. It describes the history of monotheism and the beginnings of the disclosure of the Kingdom of God on Earth.

What I want us to understand in this section of the narrative is that Israel was unique in the ancient world. The God of Israel is a totally different sort from all the other gods and religions in the ancient East. Yahweh is a "moral being who controls nature and history, and in them, reveals his righteous will and summons men to obey it."[144]

All the other major kingdoms of the ancient world had their pantheon of gods variously arranged. Only Israel had the one God, introducing monotheism to the world of religion.

Recently, I watched the National Geographic Channel (11 August 2020) on a program entitled "The Lost Treasures of Egypt." The documentary was highlighting animal mummies found protecting a human burial ground. On this particular occasion, the animal was a crocodile named Sobek, an animal god who had divine power to protect kings and pharaohs in the afterlife. They believed the Nile River was created by the sweat of these creatures.

The amazing thing to me as I watched this unfold was the same civilization who embraced this religious myth built the Pyramids of Giza within inches of tolerance to perfection—monuments still standing today. How can this be? How can they get it so wrong with religion and so right with constructing the pyramids, the only remaining monuments of the Severn Wonders of the Ancient World? It's mystifying!

Continuing on with the Nation of Israel, we can find no period in her history when Israel did not believe she was the chosen people of Yahweh. Note, this choosing took place in history. The Bible tracks this history of election back to Abraham, the father of the faith (Genesis 12:1–3), but it was in the Exodus events that Israel saw her real beginnings as a people.[145]

To summarize this section, one could say that Israel bequeathed to history and civilization four things: 1) a monotheistic religion encompassing stories, laws, covenants, songs, letters, and visions because God willingly and intentionally immersed Himself in the lives and times of His people[146]; 2) the importance of covenant (Genesis 12:1–3) with God ingratiating Himself to a people in history; 3) a linear concept of history moving toward a perfect end—a "telos" or goal,[147] and 4) the survival of an ethnic band of people who have reconfigured and are, as we speak, major players in our world. Ask yourself, why is Israel still such a major player in the world today?

Could it be because the God that called them into existence has a master plan for them and the world around them?

GOVERNMENT IN THE UNITED STATES OF AMERICA

Verna M. Hall states in the Foundation for American Christian Education, "The determining factor as to whether our nation is a Christian nation and as to whether the Constitution is a Christian document is—not whether Christians formed the Constitution—but whether *the form is Christian*. The basis for judgment is the Bible.[148]

It has been the esteemed judgment of the Founding Fathers and multitudes after them that the basis for the form of government in the United States was bathed in the Judeo-Christian worldview of life on this planet. We were conceived as a God-fearing nation because we gave deference to God in the founding documents and most of the founders could be located somewhere on the Protestant map.

The terms used in the Declaration of Independence forever enshrine language from the Old Testament. In fact, four key words formed the mosaic of the American Republic—*truth*: "we hold these truths"; *liberty*: "with certain unalienable rights, that among them are life, liberty, and the pursuit of happiness; *law:* "the laws of nature and nature's God; and *judge:* "appealing to the supreme Judge of the world for the rectitude of our intentions."

Some argue that the framers of the Constitution and Declaration of Independence were deists and took their que from the Enlightenment and the writings of John Locke, but the actual words chosen came from the Jewish Old Testament—creator, lawgiver, governor, judge, and providence are unmistakably Jewish and Bible. The reason they didn't use explicit Christian (New Testament) terms was because the different colonies were founded under different Christian inspirations (denominational loyalties) and thus avoiding a schism right off the bat. Please see Appendix A for further information on the background of the corporate history leading up to the Declaration.

Since the 243 years of the birth of our founding documents, we have entire libraries dedicated to our founding national charter. In fact, history is our ally in rediscovering what makes America so great among the nations of the world. Studying history brings truth to the surface. Truth imparts knowledge and confidence, and knowledge is power.

I want to suggest that which we have been bequeathed: liberty, freedom, and the individual dignity of the person is a prophetic record. The truth of this record is like a burning pillar in the night. It gives light and warmth and guides all to their destination safely. One could say it was almost a perfect storm of divine destiny, a perfect storm of the good, for in it was a convergence of key elements of revelation and truth, law, and religion that forged an experiment in government the likes of which the world had never seen before.

Please think deeply on the following fact. The Framers are saying in the Declaration of Independence that we are responsible to a Creator God as human beings. Rights are not given by government; they are innate by reason of our existence. Furthermore, every step in the Bible is a story of what happens in the human will. Human beings were "willed" by the Creator to choose their destinies. What will humans choose next? Liberty is the reason God made the universe. Michael Novak has said, "He wanted somewhere, one creature capable of recognizing that He had made all things, that the creation is good, and that He had extended His hand in friendship."

Our concepts and our way of life flow from these early understandings of freewill intertwined with the laws of nature and nature's God. They were not talking about nature in terms of trees, lakes, mountains, rivers, etc. They were talking about nature as in "a design or purpose of a thing." (for example, birds by nature fly, fish by nature swim). Man's distinguishing nature relates to distinctive capacities and characteristics. These include imagination, deliberation, judgment, and choice in action with a moral accountability. The ability to contemplate right and wrong and to act accordingly distinguishes man from the animals and all other life. These truths are universal and permanent. They are also self-evident, not because they are obvious but because when we understand that men have a certain nature, it becomes self-evident that all men, by sharing that nature, are equal. This, of course, has tremendous implications for how we govern.

Gleaves Whitney gives us a succinct summary of the five great principles of the American founding all around the organizing principle of "ordered liberty." Let's take a look at them as we keep in mind, they are predicated on our previous discussion earlier in this chapter.

1. Political freedom: America solved a huge problem in the human condition: the instability and indeed the danger of constitutional cycles. The main thing is to check the concentration of abuse of power through the rule of law, hence a written constitution. In addition the founders upheld popular sovereignty (turning the monarchical tradition on its head); a republican from of government expressed in a mixed constitution with checks and balances; a bill of rights to protect the individual and to guarantee equality of citizenship; civilian rule over the military; representation; regular elections; voting by private ballot rather than by shouts or by lot; rules governing the legal proceedings so that there was a judicially stable climate; and constitutionally mandated publication of the proceedings in the legislature, so people would know what their representatives were doing.

2. Economic freedom: America encouraged the development of the free market system with safeguards and great awaken-

ings, thus creating more prosperity for more human beings than anywhere else and solving the problem of famine and mass starvation. Our nation was fortunate to be colonized by the mother country where the Industrial Revolution began, where many of the settlers were Calvinists in search for material assurance they were saved, and where Adam Smith's *Wealth of Nations* was widely absorbed to change mercantile policies to free-market economies. America for the most part solved the economic problem of the masses, and thus another huge problem in the human condition.

3. Religious freedom: During the early modern era, religious wars decimated Europe. Learning from that unhappy experience, America's founders sought to avoid religious strife. America was the land where religious wars would end and true freedom of worship (or freedom not to worship) would develop. See Jefferson's and Madison's Virginia Statute of Religious Freedom. Another huge problem in the human condition—solved.

4. Social freedom: The U.S. Constitution prohibits aristocratic titles, encourages "tired…poor…huddled masses" to immigrate and through hard work strive for upward mobility, and participate in the vibrant civil society (Tocqueville).

5. America is an Idea, founded out of reflection and choice, not along racial, ethnic, or denominational lines (Hamilton, *The Federalist*, No.1). This made us unique at our founding. We adhere to the belief, the premise, that our principles are universal and good. This has given us a schizophrenic foreign policy. Sometimes we are crusaders; other times we are exemplars. Whether to pursue the mis-

sionary zeal to spread our civil gospel; or whether to show restraint—American foreign policy is the ebb and flow of these contrary impulses.[149]

In conclusion, as the Framers were drafting the Declaration of Independence, Thomas Jefferson said, "We are not a world ungoverned by the laws and the power of a superior agent. Our efforts are in His hands, and directed by it, and He will give them their effect in his own time."[150]

Let's face it; they wanted to acknowledge the God of heaven, and they desired His blessing on their undertakings. I believe the time has come again to renew our trust in the grand experiment called America.

How do we reign in the destructive forces and return our nation to its rightful destiny? The next section in this discourse should seal the deal.

THE KINGDOM OF GOD

Finally, we turn to the last section of this chapter, the lynchpin of all government. Our purpose here is to describe core elements of the Kingdom of God as it informs government in the Old Testament and government in the United States.

We begin with the priority of the Kingdom of God in Jesus' life and teaching. The reason we can talk about the priority of the Kingdom is because we have seen the priority of the King. "The word Kingdom(s) occurs 162 times in the New Testament and of those, 128 are in the four gospels alone."[151] It is the central concept in the New Testament and deserves our close attention.

Mark's gospel opens with the core emphasis of Jesus's life and the bombshell for all who have ever been students of history and live in anticipation of a better day. The key verse is Mark 1:14–15: "Now after John was arrested, Jesus came into Galilee, preaching the gospel of God, and saying, 'The time is fulfilled and the kingdom of God is at hand; repent, and believe in the gospel'" (RSV). Matthew uses the term "the kingdom of heaven," yet most scholars believe the two terms are interchangeable as do I. The onus of the concept is Jesus, the King of the Kingdom, and the witness of this kingdom is corporate touching all areas of society—the political, the social, the economic, the educational, and the judicial.

The word Kingdom is taken from two words, *king* and *domain*. Jesus is the king. Revelation 19:16 calls Him the "King of kings" and Revelation 1:5 calls Him "the ruler of kings of the earth." He called Himself a king in John 18:37. The Apostle Paul calls Him "the only Sovereign, the King of kings, and Lord of lords (1 Timothy 6:15).

As far as the *domain* is concerned, Ephesians 1:21 records Jesus as "far above all rule and authority and power and dominion, and above every name that is named, not only in this age but also in that which is to come" (RSV). In addition, Philippians 2:10–11 commands, "… every knee should bow … and every tongue confess that Jesus Christ is Lord, to the glory of God the Father." Numerous Psalms declare the rule of God over all the earth, including Psalm 96:10: "Say among the nations, The Lord Reigns" (RSV).

"Josephus, a rough contemporary of our New Testament, was a Jew who wrote in Greek and used the term 'Kingdom' (basileia) almost 500 times. In almost every case the word refers to a 'people governed by a king.'"[152] Digesting this would cause one to realize that the Kingdom of God is much larger than the Church even though the Church is the primary agent in the Kingdom.

The Kingdom encompasses all the reign of God both in heaven and on Earth. The gospel of the Kingdom of which Jesus is King and Lord must be preached to the nations and to "all creation" before the end of history (Matthew 24:14). God will provide a witness in the realm from one end to the other. This is why the authorities were so undone in Thessalonica when the apostles had come to declare this Kingdom: "These men who have turned the world upside down have come here also, and Jason has received them; and they are all acting against the decrees of Caesar, saying that there is another king, Jesus. And the people and the city authorities were disturbed when they heard this."[153]

No fence sitting here; the declaration of Jesus and those who follow Him is all inconclusive. The followers of Jesus are actually a new kind of breed in humanity. They are a "new kind of fellowship, a new community, a new people of God."[154]

Here we find a collision of light with darkness, one that is ongoing in our day as well. There is no evading the fact that the Church is counterculture.

Should we be surprised? We have a message for the unredeemed realm as well as the redeemed realm.

THE CORE MESSAGE

John the Baptist, Jesus, and His disciples preached repentance as necessary for entrance into the Kingdom (Matthew 3:2; John 3:3, 5). This "salvation" was being proclaimed to Israel first because they were Christ's own kindred in the flesh and bearers of the promises.[155] They were the "lost sheep of the house of Israel" (Matthew 10:6; 15:24). This explains why Jesus confined His ministry almost entirely to His own people, and why when He first sent out His disciples to preach, He instructed them with the same limitations.

The rulership of the Kingdom is a self-rule released from the inside, unlike the rule of the Old Covenant, which was a written code imposed from the outside. With Jesus, one winds up in a completely different destination. It's not a have to; it is a want to manifested in faith through the grace of God (Romans 3:22–26; 5:1–2; Ephesians 2:8–9). It carries with it ethical dimensions to be sure, but they are not as much a set of rules and regulations as they are a lifestyle of yieldedness to the direction of the Holy Spirit.

As I have studied the Kingdom of God concept for most of my life, I am very distressed concerning where the American Church has landed in terms of Kingdom ministry. Having been a pastor of a local church for almost forty years, I am very well-acquainted with how church operates. The entire church world is far too much like a "campus" or too "site-oriented," having developed programs and functions to keep folks busy in six embedded areas of Protestant church life: worship, evangelism, mission, discipleship, Sunday school, and pastoral care. Believe it or not, these areas are far too "in-house" in their orientation, leaving the streets empty of a real New Testament punch. In North America particularly, the program emphasis of the local church abrogates a New Testament agenda (preaching, teaching, and healing) and supplants it with a denominational agenda of busy work.

Reggie McNeil offers some poignant examples:

- The prevailing concept of church as a *place* associated with a particular set of activities—that is, an *it*, not a *who*.

- A scorecard for success based largely on church activities led by church people for church people, primarily on church property.

- A pervasive consumer mentality whereby a church congregation is evaluated on the strength and quality of its programming.

- A misguided sense of purpose—seeing "building the church" as God's primary mission in the world.

- A clergy (church leadership) trained to manage an institution (real estate, budgets, etc.) and produce religious goods and services (sermons, programs, religious rites).

- A membership trained to "give to the church" their talents, time, and treasure, and whose spirituality is assessed according to their participation in church activities, which is seen as "supporting the church."

- Church resources spent primarily on buildings, staff, and church-based programs, with much lower priority given to alleviating human need and suffering.

- Church members' expectations or assumptions that it is "the church's job" to provide spiritual training and nurture for their children.

- The inability of many church people to have in-depth conversations about God, even with their spouses and children. Instead, they have conversations about church that largely reflect consumer issues: "How did you like the service?" "What did you think of the pastor's sermon?" "Are you planning to attend the youth event this weekend?"

These are participation-in-church-activities discussions, not discipleship or spiritual-growth conversations.

- The inability of many church people to have spiritual conversations with non-church people. Church people often know how to talk about church activity, but not about God or his Kingdom priorities. People in our culture want to have God conversations, not church conversations.

- A T-shirt-and-bumper-sticker theology that says it all: "I love my church"; "Follow me to church"; "This is my church"; "A place where [fill in the blank]."[156]

The New Testament presents a much different picture.

Consider Matthew 4:23–24: "And he went about all Galilee, teaching in their synagogues and preaching the gospel of the kingdom and healing every disease and every infirmity among the people. So his fame spread throughout all Syria, and they brought him all the sick, those afflicted with various diseases and pains, demoniacs, epileptics, and paralytics, and he healed them" (RSV). The unfolding of these encounters continues in Matthew 9:35. A bit later in His journey, Jesus sent out His disciples to do exactly the same thing (Luke 10:1, 9). Furthermore, this manner of operation continued in the early Church. Here is a sampling:

- The signs of a true apostle were performed among you in all patience, with signs and wonders and mighty works (2 Corinthians 12:12).

- "And God confirmed the message by giving signs and wonders and various miracles and gifts of the Holy Spirit whenever he chose (Hebrews 2:4 NLT).

- "I ask you again, does God give you the Holy Spirit and work miracles among you because you obey the law? Of course not! It is because you believe the message you heard about Christ" (Galatians 3:5).

- "And my message and my preaching were very plain. Rather than using clever and persuasive speeches, I relied only on the power of the Holy Spirit. I did this so you would trust not in human wisdom but in the power of God" (1 Corinthians 2:4–5).

- "For when we brought you the Good News, it was not only with words but also with power, for the Holy Spirit gave you full assurance that what we said was true. ...." (1 Thessalonians 1:5).

- They were convinced by the power of miraculous signs and wonders and by the power of God's Spirit. In this way, I have fully presented the Good News of Christ from Jerusalem all the way to Illyricum" (Romans 15:18).

- "I also pray that you will understand the incredible greatness of God's power for us who believe him. This is the same mighty power that raised Christ from the dead and seated him in the place of honor at God's right hand in the heavenly realms" (Ephesians 1:19).

- "For the Kingdom of God is not just a lot of talk; it is living by God's power" (1 Corinthians 4:20).[157]

SIGNS, WONDERS, AND MIRACLES

The miracles, signs, and wonders and mighty works ("power," Greek: dunamis), were the calling card of the Church preparing the multitudes to believe the gospel. Miracle describes the manifestation of supernatural power. It actually is a flexible term describing a variety of events or happenings such as special acts of God in the natural order, e.g. storms (Exodus 14:21), earthquakes (Judges 5:4–5), volcanic activity (Exodus 14:21), and eclipse (Joel 2:20).

Other times, they include experiences of human personality such as epilepsy (Mark 9:17–27), hysteria (Mark 1:23–26; Acts 16:16–18), and demons cast out (Mark 5:1–20). Still other times, they involve spectacular phenomena believed to be either outside the process of nature or in violation of those processes as in portents, prodigies, and signs. The miracles are "powers" because they display the mighty power of God. These powers were seen through the long history of Israel and culminated in the person of Jesus Christ. (1 Corinthians 1:23–24). The word "powers" is also translated to mighty works (Matthew 7:22; Luke 10; 13; Matthew 11:20) or "miracles" in Acts 2:22 (1 Corinthians 12:10; Galatians 3:5). Additional words for miracles are great things (Luke 1:49), glorious things (Luke 13:17), strong things (Luke 5:26), wonderful things (Matthew 21:15), marvelous things (Psalms 78:12), and marvelous works (Psalm 29:12; 105:5).

In addition, the word "sign" (semeion) portrays the aspect of authenticating the miracle worker themselves. It establishes a kind of seal of God upon the person's ministry (Acts 14:5; Mark 6:30; John 10:37–38; 2 Corinthians 12:12). This was why Jesus's miracles were signs of something more, beyond themselves, especially in the Gospel of John (John 10:37-38), such as turning the water into wine (John 2:1–11) or raising Lazarus from the dead (John 11:38–44). Furthermore, the word "wonder" (teras) has to do with the state of mind produced on the eyewitnesses by the sight of a miracle. A real miracle tends to leave one "awestruck" as when Jesus commanded a storm to cease (Mark 4:41). These kinds of things just tend to burn into one's mind.

Viewing a "wonder" will strike the imagination of the viewer while pointing to a deeper meaning in the author of the miracle (Jesus). This is precisely how the gospel was presented and still today should be as the Church heals disease, defeats evil powers, exercises authority over nature, etc. When you see these things happen, the Kingdom of God is present.

Sadly, one rarely sees this prophetic witness taking place in the twenty-first century Church in America. I am calling the Church to return to its primal New Testament state and stand firm in a clear gospel witness with signs following. Only then will we see the five distinct areas of the New Testament Church come into focus in our day. Those five areas are a) conducting outreach with signs and wonders following (Matthew 9:34; 10:8); b) demonstrating victory over sin and death (John 11:25–26; Galatians2:20); c) crushing the kingdom of darkness (Luke 10:18; Matthew 12:22–28; Mark 3:24); d) making disciples (Matthew 28:16–29; Mark 16:15–18); and e) anticipating an eschatological conclusion (Acts 1:11; 1 Thessalonians 4:15–17; Titus 2:13; 1 Corinthians 15:25; Philippians 1:6; Acts 3:21).

As I muse on these five commissioned activities from Jesus to His followers, I am reminded of the phrase in the Lord's prayer: "Thy kingdom come, thy will be done." We are all being summoned to participate in the collision of light with darkness, the theological violence with the New Testament, violence as Jesus's Kingdom unfolds toward the end of time. Here is what Matthew's gospel said it would look like: "From the days of John the Baptist until now the kingdom of heaven has suffered violence, and men of violence have taken it by force" (Matthew 11:12). In other words, there is no way around a confrontation of light with darkness when adjudicating the Kingdom of God on Earth.

It's high time the government of God takes its rightful place among the kingdoms of this world. We are all being conscripted for the battle.

Reggie McNeal puts it succinctly: "The Kingdom of God is life as God intends it to be, his original blueprint for all of creation."[158]

CHAPTER 7

FORM AND ESSENCE

AS I PLUNGE INTO THIS CHAPTER, I need to be a bit autobiographical to give context to the central thought of form and essence. During my senior year of college (Ohio State University) and following a recent dramatic conversion experience to Jesus Christ, I received a definite call to ministry, the likes of which were never on the radar of my life. Interestingly enough, I literally graduated from college one day and began seminary the next.

The first day at United Theological Seminary in Dayton, Ohio (my hometown), I met a friend from the Western Pennsylvania Conference of the United Methodist Church, who became a very close friend. Early in the Fall of 1970, he took me to an interdenominational charismatic prayer meeting being held at the convent of the Precious Blood on Salem Avenue in Dayton.

Since I had driven by the Convent hundreds of times in my youth, I knew exactly where it was but never had occasion to go in. Upon entering the meeting, we observed Methodists, Presbyterians, Catholics, and Baptists all worshipping the Lord together with hands raised and smiles on their faces. I did not remember people singing with smiles on their faces at my home church in Dayton.

At nondesignated intervals, the participants would all speak in tongues (Acts 2:1–5), and prophetic words would come forth. I was unfamiliar with all of this; however, it didn't take long to realize God was all over the meeting. I realized they had something called the "baptism in the Holy Spirit."

Immediately, a longing for this experience began to rise in my life. A few weeks later, I returned to the prayer meeting, and I was baptized in the Holy Spirit and spoke in tongues. This baptism was a real shot of adrenaline, which has never ceased. I can truly say this was one of the great galvanizing moments of my entire life.[159] In deference to this experience, I will use the Charismatic renewal as a template for the following discussion of form and essence.

The next fifteen years, following my experience in the Holy Spirit, I not only studied the Charismatic renewal, but I also became a leader in it as well. Every revival or move of God has both form and essence. The Charismatic renewal was not different, however, because it was to become the most broad-based movement of the Spirit of God in history, encompassing not only the Protestant world, the Catholic Church, the Orthodox Church, the Jewish Messianic movement, and many points in-between. The Charismatic renewal will serve well to illustrate form and essence.

UNPACKING THE CONCEPT

Many people have been the benefactors of the Charismatic Renewal, having hit the denominational world in 1960 when an Episcopal priest from Van Nuys, California, was baptized in the Holy Spirit and spoke in tongues. His name was Dennis Bennett, a highly acclaimed author. I recommend his book entitled *The Holy Spirit and You*, to introduce people to the baptism in the Holy Spirit.

In the last forty years, upwards of 650 million people worldwide have joined in this great move of God. In fact, it is the largest single section of the Body of Christ on Earth other than the Roman Catholic Church. The movement brought with it the experience of the baptism in the Holy Spirit with speaking in tongues while embracing all the gifts of the Holy Spirit for empowerment.[160] It also brought with it scriptural soundness to many, many churches and ministries along with the birth of magazines, journals, and books, as well as the emergence of Bible scholars blazing a trail of the supernatural from the smallest hamlet to the largest cities in America. Many of the national leaders of the movement, including Judson Cornwall, Charles Simpson, Derek Prince, Don Basham, Bob Mumford, and Kenneth Hagin, came to our city (Columbus, Ohio) to teach and heal in the name of Jesus. This is where the concept of form comes into play.

The need for teachers and resources to help shape and steward the essence of what God was doing (pouring out His Spirit and reviving New Testament Christianity) would result in guiding the movement and blessing scores of hungry pastors and leaders who had nowhere else to go to learn about the move of God in our time. It was a really big deal.[161]

I remember vividly when Francis MacNutt, a Spirit-filled Catholic priest and leader in the movement, came to our Aldersgate National Conference on the Holy Spirit in the early 1980s. When he would get up to speak, he would first begin "singing in the Spirit" (tongues), and people all over the room would begin to be touched by God in various ways. Some would fall out of their seats, and some would yell and praise God while they were being healed of various sicknesses and disease. No one in the Protestant world had ever seen anything like this, other than Katherine Kuhlman.

Some of the antecedents of the Charismatic renewal, which are still affecting the Church today, are the concept of unity in the Body of Christ, the experience and direction of worship in the Body of Christ, and the understanding of evangelism as it relates to eschatology. I would like to look at these individually to give us a sense of the influence of the renewal across the Church.

First, the notion of unity. The Apostle Paul makes it very clear that unity among the brothers and sisters in Christ is of paramount importance. It belongs to the "in Christ" experience. Ephesians 2:14–15 (NLT) could not be more direct in this regard: "For Christ himself has brought peace to us. He united Jews and Gentiles into one people when, in his own body on the cross, he broke down the wall of hostility that separated us. He did this by ending the system of law with its commandments and regulations …."

He made peace between Jews and Gentiles by creating in Himself one new people from the two groups. In fact, this was fore-shadowed in the Old Testament in the book of Ezekiel 37:15ff, detailing God's heart to see Israel and Judah come together as one. It would be worth your time to pause now and read this text be-cause it is a message seen throughout the Bible and the twenty-first century, which I believe could be the final laboratory.

In addition, the Apostle Paul had many things to say on the subject of unity. Please observe the following admonitions: 1 Cor-inthians 1:10, Philippians 1:27, and Philippians 2:2. Add to these the following petitions from Jesus's prayer as recorded in John 17:20–24: "I do not pray for these only, but also for those who be-lieve in me through their word, that they may all be one … so that the world may believe that they may be one even as we are one that they may become perfectly one, so that the world may know ...." Add to these the famous words on unity in Psalm 133:1–2: "Behold, how good and pleasant it is when brothers dwell in unity! It is like the precious oil upon the head, running down upon the beard, upon the beard of Aaron, running down on the collar of his robes!" (RSV),

Having studied the above composite picture in light of the Charismatic renewal, one could see no greater consequence in our lifetime for affecting unity than the outworking of the renewal. In the world, differences in people inevitably produce division in practice. Because of this, a democratic form of government where people agree to abide by the majority vote is probably the best that can be expected this side of heaven. However, the Church is not a loosely knit assemblage of people, each doing their own thing and moving ahead by compromising with one another. No, the Church is intended to be a living organism called together by the Holy Spirit and carrying out the will of Jesus who is the head.

Therefore, Jesus said in John 14:15–16, "If you love me, you will keep my commandments. And I will pray the Father, and he will give you another Counselor, to be with you for ever" (RSV). Jesus was the initial counselor spending three years of intensive life with the disciples, but the Holy Spirit given at Pentecost would literally be experienced by those who believe from all over the world. In other words, the Holy Spirit can produce in all who are submitted to Him a unity of heart (a common affection), a unity of mind (a common understanding), and a unity of will (a common commitment to action).

In Columbus, upon recognizing these truths, we started a citywide pastors' network called "The Capital City Association of Ministers and Churches," which served the Greater Columbus

Area from the mid-1980s to 2018, when it morphed into an apostolic network. I have been privileged to lead both networks for many years. We recognized as did the New Testament, that all believers in a city or area were really one body meeting in many places. God's intent was that they know one another and work together in unity, not in competition.

The challenge is always how to hold on to the vision—the essence while being open to new forms. It is so easy to miss it when we are holding on to familiar forms.

Someone had said, "The greatest enemy of the next move of God is the last move of God."

At times, we hold tightly to form, mistaking it for essence.

NATIONAL AND INTERNATIONAL UNITY

Moving from a citywide unfolding to a national and international form has also been facilitated by the presence of the Charismatic renewal. Father Peter Hocken, a Catholic priest and leader in the renewal says, "The claim that the basic spiritual reality being called the baptism in the Holy Spirit is fundamentally the same grace across all the different church groupings imported by the charismatic movement."[162] He continues, "The church needs such movements to shake it up, to challenge all forms of immobility and stagnation, and to unleash fresh dynamism from the Spirit of God."[163]

Many years ago, I was on the organizing committee for an ecumenical Spirit-filled conference held in the Louisiana Superdome in 1987. There were 40,000 people in attendance, 20,000 of whom were Roman Catholic. Father Hocken said of this event, "The body of Christ in North America has been given a unity or a communion at the level of the Spirit which becomes a spring-board for the task of achieving a unity at the level of mind (articulated faith), leading to a level of embodied community."[164] In other words, coming together can produce serious momentum to advance the Kingdom of God on Earth.

When we expand this to the international level, we are seeing this play out in thousands of different scenarios with churches, denominations, and streams of worship for the greater good. For example, of the 1.3 billion Catholics, 120 million are charismatic; of the 400 million Pentecostals in the world, 80 million are Anglicans, 80 million are Chinese house church Christians; 80 million North Americans who identify with the Renewal; 62 million Nigerians; 39 million Filipinos; and 29 million Democratic Republic of Congo Christians.[165]

It bears witness by saying the original Charismatic renewal (1960–1990) was a form which served another time. The future will require new forms, but the essence is the same. We will consider some of these new forms as we proceed. However, the essence of any revival is a life-changing encounter with the power and presence of God through the Holy Spirit. There is no substitute here because the Holy Spirit never becomes obsolete. New generations bring new forms which will interface with the technological tsunami enveloping the world of communication and commerce. The Church must and will accommodate itself to these new forms, which brings us to our next emphasis: music.

THE FORM OF MUSIC

I realize the whole area of music is a minefield in the contemporary church. There are probably as many opinions and tastes as there are people. But music is a form, and like other forms, will evolve and change over time as it serves the purpose of God.

In the early days of the renewal, God gave birth to what was known as Scripture songs taken directly from the Bible, many of which were right out of the Psalms. The songs were simple, easy to remember and sing, plus easy to play on the piano or guitar. They were also plentiful, so much so that the hymnbook became a "loose-leaf" notebook in many instances because songs could literally be added weekly. The form from these songs suited the overall atmosphere in those days, which was the joy of the Lord. I, for one, am grateful for this legacy, and still on occasion, enjoy singing those choruses, many of which are indelibly imprinted on my mind.

I remember well changing hymnbooks in my denominational church a few years after my arrival (June 1973). This was a big decision for a local church because in most cases, they would be committing themselves to a form for years to come.

Following a thorough study, we decided to purchase "Hymns for the Family of God," produced by the Church of God in Anderson, Indiana. The hymnal included praise choruses by people like Jack Hayford, Bill Gaither, and others, reflecting the music of the day. Some of these choruses could be sung over several times as the Holy Spirit would penetrate deeper with each successive round.

This hymnal, along with a Spirit-filled pianist, completely changed the atmosphere during a Sunday morning service. Soon after, we started a Sunday evening service where we could really pull out the stops and use the "loose-leaf" book along with an overhead projector. The combinations were endless. Worshippers didn't even have to hold a book, which freed them to raise their hands in worship.

The above form will not reach a young generation of today, who are computer savvy and embossed with social media platforms. Just as society has grown more multifacted and diverse, so has the music that reflects it. Today, the songs are longer, the music more complex, the beat tilts toward a rock style, spastic at times and very loud. But it is the form God is using today.

If the Church can stay ahead of the curve with music, she will remain relevant to a generation, not only very diverse ethnically, but also fragmented by divorce, single-parent homes, and dissonant in cultural values.

I believe God is raising up a generation of musicians and worship leaders to carry and spread the anointing of the Holy Spirit (essence), which fueled a worldwide Charismatic renewal, only now twenty-first century style. They have a heart to worship and are all in for Jesus. They value authenticity and loath hype and ego-related platforms. God is still faithful to "a thousand generations," never releasing us from the palm of His hand.

I took quite a bit of heat from my colleagues in ministry back in the day (1970s to mid-1980s) for the form and style of music we were enjoying. They used to ask, "Are you hanging from the chandeliers yet?"

But in time, these same churches adopted what was known as "contemporary worship" in their own services. They were forced to embrace the new kind of worship or witness a significant exodus of people from their church.

Somehow, I was always ahead of the curve in the local church allowing us to never grow stale in the area of worship. In fact, it became the determining factor to attract new blood into the fellowship. Along with the Spirit-filled worship came the power of God, the prophetic in the gathered assembly, healing, and miracles. One never knew what exactly was going to happen on a given Sunday.

Charles Wesley wrote over 5,000 hymns in the eighteenth century, and the Wesleyan revival was born on the wings of those songs, many of which came right out of the secular culture yet saturated with Christian theology. Today, the music is contemporaneously governed by churches like Bethel in Redding, California, and Gateway Church in the Dallas-Fort Worth area with their worldwide Gateway music ministry. Robert Morris, the pastor of Gateway Church, had a dream one night in 1993, which became a vision for ministry. The word in the dream was "I want to build a church of thirty thousand people that reaches three hundred thousand in the Dallas-Fort Worth Metroplex. I also want the church to reach three million people in Texas, thirty million people in America, and three hundred million people around the world."[166] This could only happen through the amazing proliferation of music generated from their multi-campus complex.

Their music is no hype, no manipulation, no appealing to ego or glory, just letting God do His thing through yielded Spirit-empowered vessels. By the way, music has always preceded and enveloped great moves of God in history. We are seeing it before our eyes in the day we live in. The Kingdom of God will come in a demonstration of the Spirit and power, while light dispels darkness.

In all our music and outreach, let's keep the essence of what God has done while being open to new forms to expose and guide the next outpouring for the days ahead. I have full assurance that the Lord of Glory will indeed continue to speak to His church in relevant ways as we approach the end of history.

EVANGELISM AND THE WORLDWIDE INGATHERING

The book of Joel quoted by the Apostle Peter in Acts 2 speak of those who will be gathered into the Kingdom of God during the outpouring of the latter days. Joel says, "Multitudes, multitudes, in the valley of decision! For the day of the Lord is near in the valley of decision."[167] As we consider these words of Joel, new far-reaching forms of evangelism are being conducted as we speak.

I serve on the Global Council of an international outreach effort known as Empowered21. It is being coordinated out of Oral Roberts University with their president Billy Wilson at the helm. The Empower 21 movement is a worldwide conglomerate of Christian assemblies dedicated to passing on the DNA of the Charismatic renewal to the next-gen disciples in the Body of Christ by "connecting generations for intergenerational blessing and impartation." Scores of young people are being summoned to pray and act as agents of the Holy Spirit to reach their own generation as well. The effort is being unfurled throughout the globe by dividing the earth into fourteen different sections, each with its own council and coordinating activities of evangelism.

The vision of Empowered21 is to see that "every person on earth would have an authentic encounter with Jesus Christ through the power and presence of the Holy Spirit by Pentecost 2033." This will happen through networks of Christian leaders wedded to regions of the world experiencing a coordinated effort to win yet-unreached groups to the Lord Jesus. It is without question the biggest undertaking I have ever been involved in.

The Global Council meets yearly at points all over the world to receive progress reports from the fourteen regions and to coordinate and inspire efforts under way. The Council is divided into four main sections—the Council itself, a scholar's track that studies a given topic and produces a book each year to help resource the larger church worldwide; a global alliance of evangelists; and a world-prayer effort to pray for every person on the planet by 2033. The year 2033 will be the two-thousandth birthday of Pentecost, and adherents want to ramp up to the big celebration by beginning to celebrate Pentecost in the local church on par with how we celebrate Christmas and Easter.

A second effort being explored with broad implications for evangelism in America is called "All America." This is an initiative of the "Call to All" movement (Mark Anderson), mobilizing the Body of Christ in America to focus and collaborate in an effort to fulfill the Great Commission within the boundaries of our fifty states (Matthew 28:16–20). Their philosophy is that America is under judgment but has been given a reprieve in order to call the nation to repentance using the same aggressive strategies formerly used oversees while applying them to America.

To illustrate how form and essence is working here, an App (All America) has been developed to track every home in the nation,[168] which will be adopted by willing participants. Their desire is to connect every person in America with the gospel until all 127 million households and every school campus is adopted. To realize this, they will take people across "five finish lines": a) pray for the household (neighbor) by name; b) develop a personal relationship with your neighbor c) introduce them to the Bible; d) introduce them to Jesus Christ as Savior and Lord; and e) connect them to a church or Christian fellowship where they can grow and be discipled in the faith. I am personally involved in this effort in my city and help to give leadership to an area-wide effort in Columbus, Ohio.

The internet has opened up a whole new world for commercialization, including access to communication modalities which affect the work of God's Church on earth. I say this because in my lifetime, it seems that the Church has always been many years behind societal innovations. However, with computers and the internet, the Church has been forced to jump into the fray or be severely left behind. As a result, progress in evangelism and unity in the Body of Christ have opened up a whole new world of ministry, to the point of actually closing the Great Commission in our lifetime.

The day of the mass crusade (Billy Graham, Louis Palau) have been replaced with online modalities to reach far more people with the click of a mouse or a function on your cell phone. The essence is the same, but the forms have changed.

This effort could not have been done twenty years ago, but the availability of these technologies have brought the future to our doorstep. All we need now are laborers for the harvest. These and many other efforts carry the essence of mission and evangelism into the twenty-first century with new forms to accompany them.

A cursory glance at history demonstrates to the casual observer how God has always been "reinventing" the Church to remain relevant to His purpose in history. From the desert fathers in the fifth and sixth centuries; to the monastic movement during the Dark Ages when worker bees cloistered away in monasteries copying manuscripts of the Bible by hand so as to preserve the Word of God for the ongoing Church prior to the invention of the printing press; to the Protestant Reformation with its emphasis on saving grace and the priesthood of the believer; to the camp meetings and revival movements of the eighteenth and nineteenth centuries, blazing a trail of disciples to Jesus while the nation expanded westward; to the twentieth century with its conglomerate of denominations and ecumenical collaborations including the Charismatic renewal, we have seen the hand of God.

While the Church has been ever changing its forms, the essence has remained.

Today, it is our turn, and God is not finished yet. We must keep our hands to the plow and our ears to heaven to resist and repel the efforts of secular culture. The '60s radicals have done a good job at changing their forms while retaining the essence of their ideology–impacting our society to the extent of bringing our entire nation to the brink of socialism.

I am sorry to say the Church at-large has been too splintered with diversity, doctrine, disunity, and distraction to stop their movement. It goes well-beyond culture wars at this point. We are now being guided by the unseen hand of God to prepare for an end-times witness and final harvest.

So, to this subject, we now turn for our conclusion. Are you ready?

CHAPTER 8

AN END-TIMES CHURCH AT MIDNIGHT

IN STUDYING THE HISTORY OF THE CHURCH, I can see three great world religious epochs, one of which I believe we may have already entered. The first epoch was initiated by the promise God made to Abraham in Genesis 12 and reiterated again later to receive a family as vast as "the stars of heaven, and the sands of the seashore."[169] This, of course, after 400 years, was issued in the birth of the nation of Israel, along with a clear witness to the ancient world of the existence of a monotheistic faith.

The second epoch was initiated by the birth, life, death, and resurrection of Jesus Christ as the fulfilment of a prophetic destiny and universal salvation for all who come to Him: "… To him who loves us and has freed us from our sins by his blood and made us a kingdom, priests to His God and Father …." (Revelation 1:5–6).[170]

The third and final epoch is revealed with the latter days Church (Isaiah 59:21; Acts 2:38–39), who will live in and witness the events described in the book of Revelation. However, an important caveat is that the first two epochs are hundreds of years long, while the third epoch, by comparison, is brief.

We do not know the day or the hour of the coming of the Lord, but we do know the season because the Bible makes it clear that certain "signs" will prevail as we approach the end of the age and those "signs" are already at hand.

The biblical markers for such a season will be plain to see: deceptions, wars and rumors of wars, famines, pestilences, earthquakes, anti-Christ movements, betrayals, increased hatred, false prophets, lawlessness, increased in satanic influence, and the gospel will be preached to the whole world (ethne).

EMPOWER WORLD CONGRESS 2020

Bishop Ken Ulmer (Faithful Central Bible Church, Los Angeles), in a virtual address to the Empowered21 World Congress in June 2020 said, "God does not do anything unless he tells his servants the prophets" (Amos 3:7).

Prophets see from peak to peak; pastors generally see from valley to valley. The pastor is called to walk with the faithful in their life's trials and challenges, The prophet, on the other hand, issues a clarion call to what God is doing in the present/future.

Into this eschatological mix, there will be a generation who lives and witnesses the last days' events. They are described in the Bible as a "Bride" adorning herself for her Bridegroom, Jesus.[171] The Bride will know where she is at in the prophetic history just as Anna, Simeon, Elizabeth, Mary mother of Jesus, Herod, John the Baptist, Zacharias, and the Wise men from Persia knew the time of their calling. These people had a prophetic understanding of the timeline of God's unfolding plan as well as cognition of their role. God will not leave His people without a witness.

I believe the church is even now waking up to see what God is doing in the earth in these latter days and final hours of human history. In a passage of scripture from Isaiah, the prophet is describing a day coming when God will grow a Branch from an old stump (David), and the Branch will bear the fruit of righteousness and truth (Is.11:5). Almost all scholars believe this to be pointing to Jesus Christ. Then the prophet goes on to say a few verses later, "Nothing will hurt or destroy in all my holy mountain, for as the water fills the sea, so the earth will be filled with people who know the Lord" (Isaiah 11:9 NLT). Concerning this verse, Dan Juster says, "I believe that the implication here is that the whole world would be baptized in the Holy Spirit.[172]

Friends, we are literally seeing this with the 650 million baptized Christians described earlier in the previous chapter.

It's time to wake up, we are in momentous days.

Bishop Ulmer reminds us that the worse place to be is where God used to be. Ouch! If we spend our days going back to yesterday, we will miss where God is going tomorrow. There is no new normal for the Church. There is only the present unfolding revelation as per His apostles and prophets. God is saying, in essence, "If you go back to yesterday, you are going to miss me; I am doing a new thing."[173] I mean a brand-new thing, so don't miss it!

God is about to release a new end-times faith expression which can only be recognized and lived in an end-times environment. Furthermore, this will come without a point of reference because we have never gone this way before. We can surely take our que from Pentecost, when the 120 gathered at Jesus's request in the Upper Room to pray—they did not know what to expect in terms of how it would unfold. They only knew to "wait" until they were "clothed with power from on high," filling them with boldness for the next leg of the journey (Luke 24:49).

I believe we are at a place in history that would mirror Pentecost, only being enfolded in the last-days scenario. And make no mistake about it—God is alerting His Church worldwide for the great climax.

So we would do well to pay attention every day we wake up and go about our day. Let me use the analogy of driving a car. Which portion of the glass are you going to use the most, the rear-view mirror or the windshield? If you pay too much attention to the rearview mirror, you will crash the car. (I could throw the cell phone in as well). You must spend all of your time looking through the windshield to navigate your direction and destination. In other words, we cannot go back in life. We must go forward in the day we are given (Matthew 6:34).

God is pouring out His Spirit today like never before in history. With the advent of the internet and the smartphone, the world is connected like never before (Daniel 12:4). We know instantly about events that happen on the other side of the world. It's a set-up for the end-times Church.

My friends, I will say it again. Let us work while it is day, for the night cometh when no man can work.

YET ONCE MORE

"His voice then shook the earth; but now he has promised, 'Yet once more I will shake not only the earth but also the heaven.' This phrase, 'Yet once more,' indicates the removal of what is shaken, as of what has been made, in order that what cannot be shaken may remain." (Hebrews 12:26–27 RSV).

I believe this verse is instructive for us in the last days. It speaks to those who are tethered to the Kingdom of God on Earth. So much of the time we concentrate on the "shaking" part of the sentence, when really the more important part is the "what remains that cannot be shaken."

God is making room for the clear, visible outworking of His presence and agenda in the world right now. Things are coming apart so that things can come together.

Keith Green had a song in the late '60s called "Asleep in the Light." Its haunting message is the world is not being reached and is asleep in the dark because the Church is asleep in the light.

The shaking that is coming will wake up many who are asleep in the light. Furthermore, the glue that is going to hold us together in this coming "unveiling" of God will be our relational identity, not our branding.

The true Church will be in fellowship and prefer one another over the panic and chaos that will surely come with the shaking.

THE MIDNIGHT CRY

A few years ago, one of the leaders in our city was heading a study tour to Israel. When they arrived at the check-in counter in New York to board the plane, the ticket agent looked at Brondon's passport and said, "You're not going anywhere. Your passport has expired."

Stunned, he couldn't believe it. Sure enough, it was expired. So, he had to stay in New York an extra day to get his passport renewed at the American Consulate while he sent the team on to Israel to wait for him to arrive a day late.

Brondon shared, "I asked the Lord why He didn't tell me. He said, 'I did, but you were too busy doing and going for you to hear Me.'"

The problem was that the time he applied for the passport and the date that it expired was so long (ten years), that he forgot about it.

Then Brondon said: "He [God] told me at the end of the age, people will be doing ministries, great things for Him, but they will not know the passport of their heart has expired. And the length of time between when He says He is coming and when He comes causes us to forget that. It's our hearts that He wants, not the stuff we are doing for Him."

We've got to start talking about His coming because it reminds us, He's coming. It helps to remind us to keep our hearts right and to get them right if they're not right. When we don't talk about His coming, we basically set ourselves up to miss His coming.

If we are not expecting His return, we are not preparing for His return. It is that simple.

The Bible warns us of the danger of being lukewarm. That is why the Spirit says, "Today when you hear his voice, don't harden your hearts as Israel did when they rebelled, when they tested me in the wilderness" (Hebrews 3:7–8 NLT). So much of the Church today is lukewarm, similar to the people of Israel's rebellion in the wilderness.

R.T. Kendall, a very popular contemporary author, wrote the book *Prepare Your Heart for the Midnight Cry*.[174] It's an exposition and interpretation of the parable of the ten virgins in Matthew 25:1–13. I found it to be a well-thought-out and frankly, a frightening view of future events about to come upon an unsuspecting world.

In the parable, the ten virgins typify the regenerate people of God. These are the ones eligible to go into the marriage feast, but even at that, they were not all totally prepared.

A closer look will help us focus in on the core meaning. First, they were all virgins (purity). These women were set aside for a purpose. Secondly, they all had oil (the Spirit) in their lamps (John 6:63). So they belonged to Him. Their eventual problem was that they did not pursue the Spirit so that they would have enough oil to complete the experience. In other words, not all of us who are saved pursue Him with diligence so that we know and walk with Him intimately.

How can we guard against being lulled to sleep?

- by walking in the light (1 John 1:7)

- by resisting temptation (James 1:12)

- by not grieving the Holy Spirit (Ephesians 4:30)

And third, they all fell asleep. Jesus continually warned His disciples, "stay awake." Mark 13:35–37 enjoins us to "Watch therefore—for you do not know when the master of the house will come, in the evening, or at midnight, or at cockcrow, or in the morning—lest he come suddenly and find you asleep. And what I say to you I say to all: Watch" (RSV).

Brother Kendall reminds us of a few things about sleep: 1) We don't know we are asleep until we wake up. 2) We do things in our sleep that we would not do when we are awake. 3) We hate the sound of an alarm (e.g. Ground Hog Day).

In addition, expectancy would greatly help this entire process. Jesus's second coming is called the "blessed hope" (Titus 2:13). Expectancy is not only important, it is essential. It is the way that God wants us to live.

Robert Mapes Anderson says in his book *Vision of the Disinherited*, "The consistently dominant theme of the early Pentecostal movement was 'Jesus is coming soon.'"[175] (p.96) It was a nearly universal notion during the first few years of the movement. Furthermore, Charles Parham's interest was focused almost exclusively on eschatology—doctrines of the end of the world and the future state of the soul.[176]

The very first issue of the Azusa Street Mission Paper quoted, "Many are the prophecies spoken in unknown tongues and many the visions that God is giving concerning His soon coming."[177]

Consider these Scriptures in light of expectance. Psalm 130:5–6, "I wait for the Lord, my soul waits, and in his word I hope: my soul waits for the Lord more that watchman for the morning, more than watchmen for the morning."[178] Further, the Psalmist says, "Behold, as the eyes of servants look to the hand of their master, as the eyes of a maid to the hand of her mistress, so our eyes look to the Lord our God, till he has mercy on us."[179]

Add to these Scriptures on watchfulness:

- Matthew 24:42, "Watch therefore, for you do not know on what day your Lord is coming."[180]

- 2 Peter 3:10, "But the day of the Lord will come like a thief ..."

- 1 Thessalonians 5:2, "For you yourselves know well that the day of the Lord will come like a thief in the night."-Revelation 16:15, "Lo, I am coming like a thief! Blessed is he who is awake, keeping his garments that he may not go naked and be seen exposed."

- Revelation 22:17, "The Spirit and the Bride say, 'Come!' And let him who hears say, 'Come!'" There is a definite "love thing" going on between the Lord and the bride here. Prayer "cry" is integral to His coming.

Finally, Brother Kendall says in his book, "The midnight cry will coincide with a major catastrophe in the world that will exceed the event of 9/11 in terror, damage, and loss of lives." A word from the "messengers" will come within hours before or after this horrible event. This catastrophe will give great credibility to the message of the messengers.[181]

There will also be signs in the heavens at the same time. Millions will be shaken rigid from head to toe, falling on their faces, hiding—if possible—-from the wrath of the Lamb."[182] To be sure, there will be several "pressures" converging simultaneously while humanity negotiates a tumultuous time ramping up to the end of history. These will include: God's Judgement (Is. 26:19-20; 2 Thess.1:5-8) while the righteous bow and return to a renewed hope in true justice; Satan's Rage (Jn. 17:15-17; Rev. 18:1-8) while the righteous resist the devil, through a consecrated life of prayer and fasting; Creations Groan (Ro. 8:22-24; Acts 2:20; Is. 61:4) while the righteous are found rebuilding former devastations; Man's Sin (2Thess. 2:1-12) while the righteous resist the deuteriation of cultural darkness.

In addition, what can we do to prepare for the midnight cry? Scripture, as always, is our guide. Thy this:

a. Stay alert (Mark 13:35; Luke 12:35)

b. Give all diligence to make sure you have plenty of oil in your lamp to be equally pursuing the Word of the Spirit (Matthew 25:1–13)

c. Read the Bible daily with care (Ezra 7;10; 2 Timothy 1:15)

d. Spend as much time in prayer as you can daily (James 4:7)

e. Walk in all the light God gives you (1 John 1:7)

f. Be careful to walk in total forgiveness (Matthew 18:21-22); g) Maintain sexual purity—only within marriage (Proverbs 5:18).

I would encourage you to post these bullets in the back of your Bible, or put them on the refrigerator. Keep them before you.

CHRONOS VS. KAIROS TIME

Time is a key concept in the New Testament to understand the unfolding of God in history and the events leading up to the last days. Evangelist Guy Chevreau spoke in my church (Trinity Family Life Center) in Pickerington, Ohio, on June 22, 1997. It had been only a few years after the great Toronto outpouring which was still going strong at that time. Guy regularly taught at Toronto leading up to the revival and following the move of God as well. He was a Baptist who got "tampered with by the Holy Spirit."

On the Sunday morning when he spoke at Trinity, he explained the concepts of Chronos and Kairos using the analogy of a clock approaching midnight. He said it was not yet midnight, but we were most likely between the hour of 11 p.m. and midnight.

You see the Greeks had two words for time: Chronos and Kairos. "Chronos is clock time, calendar time: 1 o'clock, 2 o'clock, 3 o'clock; January, February, March...all marching right along."[183]

The second Greek word used for time was Kairos. "Those who are mothers know the difference between Chronos and Kairos." The soon-to-be mother who is nine months pregnant shakes her husband in the middle of the night and says, "It's time!" He opens a bleary eye, looks at the clock, and says, "It's 3:17 in the morning. Go back to sleep.'"[184] At that point, she is talking Kairos time, and he is still on Chronos time. "No!" she says. "IT'S TIME!"

It is important for us to grasp this concept, especially in the days we are living in. Kairos time has a connotation of pregnancy about it; something is always brought to birth. In the Gospel of Mark, what is brought to birth is the presence and the power of the Kingdom of God made known in Jesus in His preaching and His ministry."[185] Jesus is talking about a final state where something has arrived and been brought to completion (Mark 1:15).

The future that the prophets of old had spoken about had arrived. When Jesus read Isaiah 61 in the Synagogue, Kairos had kicked in.,[186] This is why Luke quotes Jesus saying, "For I tell you that many prophets and kings desired to see what you see, and did not see it, and to hear what you hear, and did not near it."[187]

John Lennox in his excellent book *Against the Flow* does give us a caution when speaking of the end of time and the last days.

"Throughout the centuries there has been a constant danger of people failing to heed Christ's warning (Luke 21:8–9). They thought that their time was the end of time, a mistake that often led to behavior which discredited the Christian message. During the Second World War, for instance, there were those who thought the activity of Hitler and Mussolini was evidence that the end times had come. But they were wrong."[188]

I realize we cannot be dogmatic on this very important issue; however, I still maintain that God will give the collective Church the thumbs up when Kairos time has initiated the approaching hoofbeats of the four horsemen of the apocalypse (Revelation 6).

I simply cannot image the Church being caught off guard in such an important time of history. Having said that, I also realize that Jesus's answer to those in His day who wanted to know the time of His appearing was not to give them days and hours on the calendar. His Word was to "be ready."

Perhaps God will mark us as He did in Ezekiel 9:4, a marked people. "And the Lord said to him, 'Go through the midst of the city, through Jerusalem, and put a mark on the foreheads of the men who sigh and groan over all the abominations that are committed in it.'"[189]

What was wrong? The city "was swollen with murder and bloated with injustice."

Friends, we are there in 2020. Our cities are burning, the moral fabric of society is collapsing, fear abounds over Coronavirus, our national debts are almost at our national revenue, never before experienced in our history as a nation. By all indications, our nation has experienced a severe moral regression. Perhaps our ship of state has collided with a deadly iceberg. It is limping badly, and there are not enough lifeboats to accommodate everyone.

It seems to me, the true mark of God on the Church in this desperate hour will be a church desperate to be healed. George Otis Jr. says in a recent blog post, "Before a nation can be healed (1 Chronicles 7:14), it must be awakened. And this can only happen if and when the Church is revived.

To realize revival, we as believers must be willing to own up to our folly, rebellion, and apathy, and humble ourselves."[190] The Church must return to her moorings. I am encouraged with all the prayer ramping up to the current presidential election just days away. Whatever candidate is elected, if we cease the prayer effort, we will most assuredly go down with the ship. If God were to mark us in New Testament terms, perhaps it would be the "fruit of the Spirit" (Galatians 5:22–24) wedded to a 2 Chronicles 7:14 lifestyle ongoing.

No doubt, these people will stand out like a sore thumb in the composite chaos of 2020.

God, mark us for Your glory in these last days. Amen!

CHAPTER 9

A CLARION CALL TO A PROPHETIC DESTINY

IN THE PREVIOUS CHAPTER, WE ENDED WITH an under-standing of how God's timing relates to the end of time as we know it. In bringing things to a conclusion, I believe it has been given to us to ready those around us for what the theology calls "the con-summation of the ages."

Perhaps we are the generation to welcome the coming of the Lord. If not, we are certainly the ones to announce it and prepare people to receive it.

We are not entering a melancholy period of history. Rather, we are in store for a lot of fireworks, social turmoil, and world-wide divine judgment, which should stimulate the Church and the world to respond with faith in Christ. The prophet Joel declares that there will be "multitudes in the valley of decision."[191] Someone said there is going to be a rude awakening before there is a great awakening. Striking news from around the world will continue to escalate and intensify until Christ returns.

Taking this into consideration, the Church of Jesus Christ is preparing for a heightened and deepened witness to Christ than has been previously expressed. Today, we are witnessing more martyrs for the Kingdom of God than at anytime in history. Just as a year is longer than a day, so the season of grace (the Church Age) has been longer than the season of judgment at the end. Before the "day of the Lord," there will be "days of the Lord" leading up to the final day.

Many believe the COVID-19 virus is part of the picture. Think about it; millions of people will have entered eternity prematurely and for what—the sin of mankind protecting his own turf?

We celebrate God's definitive act of justice and truth in the world through the life, death, and resurrection of Jesus Christ, who is our hope, our song, and our daily provision in the Spirit. Because of this, we have a stability that cannot be moved.

Ours is a long and wide look at the events that shape history. We know that nothing man does will ultimately be able to sabotage God's purpose for our lives and for history itself. There is a governing authority that will have the last word. Sin and evil will be judged, and righteousness and truth will be rewarded. This will be manifested in a process to is to "… work out your own salvation with fear and trembling, for God is at work in you both to will and to work his good pleasure."[192] The conclusive action of this process is found in 1 Thessalonians 4:16: "For the Lord himself will descend from heaven with a cry of command, with the archangel's call, and with the sound of the trumpet of God" (RSV). "And then the lawless one will be revealed, and the Lord Jesus will slay him with the breath of his mouth and destroy him by his appearing and his coming."[193] This, my friends, should be worth shouting about.

If we are indeed approaching this final Chiros epoch, then we the Church have work to do, and it will likely be a "forerunner" in nature. Begin the shout!

The day of prophetic preparation is upon us. As we have said earlier, many have identified the Church's witness in these days as a forerunner spirit. After all, we are a prophetic people, here to proclaim, to announce, and to declare.

The biblical theme of a forerunner people construes a spate of prophetic heralds who are sent ahead to announce the coming visitation of the King to a town or village. For example, in 2 Chronicles 30:5–6, the people were instructed to prepare for one of the holiest days on the Jewish calendar: Passover. Here we read: "So they decreed to make a proclamation throughout all Israel, from Beersheba to Dan, that the people should come and keep the passover to the Lord the God of Israel, at Jerusalem; for they had not kept it in great numbers as prescribed. So couriers sent throughout all Israel and Judah with letters from the king and his princes, as the king had commanded, saying, 'O people of Israel, return to the Lord, the God of Abraham, Isaac, and Israel, that he may turn again to the remnant of you who have escaped from the hand of the kings of Assyria.'"[194]

I believe God will settle for nothing less than the full attention of the twenty-first-century Christian Church.

HISTORICAL CONTEXT

As we peer into these truths, I want us to review the amazing "timing" of God in history so as to encourage us in our journey to the end. Just prior to and during the birth of Jesus into the world, so many things were popping at the same time—signs, wonders, miracles, and timing.

Let's consider timing first. The Bible says in Galatians 4:4 that Jesus came in the fullness of time. When one considers the historical context, those words become amazingly true. Take for instance the transportation system of the ancient world. The Romans had paved the way for the gospel message to be taken to Asia, Europe, and Africa through the extensive highway system they had developed. It is no secret that the Roman highways were the finest in the world, and some are still in existence today.

Furthermore, the Greek culture had provided a universal language for communicating the gospel. In the year 300 BC, a community of Greek-speaking Jewish scholars in Alexandria translated a Greek version of the Old Testament known as the Septuagint. It is abbreviated by the symbol LXX, which is seventy, because there were seventy scholars on the project.

Considering this, the New Testament writers completed their work within sixty years of the crucifixion of Jesus. This was done in an age when literature was flourishing, so to speak. Copies were made constantly, so much so that today we have 15,000 complete manuscripts and quotations of the New Testament from the era. The Bible you carry today is not a compilation of guesswork. It is the manuscript as passed down from the originals.[195]

Taking the idea of timing a little further, it was the Jewish people who were the custodians of the Scriptures the spreading the hope of a coming redeeming King. The expectation of a messiah was ripe and full under the oppressive regime of the Roman occupation. It had been 400 years since the prophets and Israel were desperate to hear from God. Here is the kicker—when Jesus arrived, they knew what they were looking for; unfortunately, they were so inwardly focused, they missed the big picture.

They wanted a military victory, and that was the end of it! Their Messiah would lead the charge. I believe this is a prophetic word for the Church today. Some have figured it out to the last minute and detail, their minds being made up. Others say, "Que sera, sera(whatever will be, will be.)"[196] Both perspectives are incorrect. Instead, the end-times Church will be found prophetically anticipating the dawn of a new heaven and Earth as the book of Revelation has described while holding to a purity of lifestyle and bold uncompromising witness, including martyrdom to the end.

The last days Church will have to reinvent herself to negotiate a demitted world culture.

REINVENTING THE CHURCH

When Jesus left the planet, the people of God were in the process of reinventing themselves in order to reach a multideistic Greek Hellenistic world. They had the cargo ("the good news") but needed the design to transport the cargo to the ancient world. The mission was evangelism (and still is), and Jesus left the Church with a powerful call to be sent, hence the apostelline.

The apostles would carry to a hostile world the healing love and salvation of Jesus. They were the *ekklesia*, the called-out ones. One gained entrance into the community of believers whenever they were convinced that you held their values and were born from above.

Think with me for a moment. These early Jewish Christians were reinventing themselves, moving from a traditional Jewish expression with priests in a hierarchical form—temple worship, sacramental rites of circumcision, etc. Yet the Church was moving into a multidimensional expression that needed to be highly mobile and adaptable to a variety of cultures and languages. They were impelled to shed some of the old trappings. Sounds contemporary to me. So, they were asking themselves, *Are we going to be Jewish or not? Are we going to practice circumcision or not? Are we going to worship in the temple or in homes?* They had to reinvent themselves. The old template was just not going to work.

To further complicate matters, the world they were sent into was hostile toward them, requiring great sacrifice, and in some cases, the ultimate sacrifice. Each group of Christians was an illicit community. There were instances when consorting with a Christian was a capital offense.

And yet they were to reach out to their neighborhood and beyond. They were instructed to be in the world but not of the world. They didn't have the luxury of playing it safe. The front door of their house was the mission field. They called it "witnessing," a word for "martyr."

Entering the Christian community was a dramatic event. This was the picture for the first 300 years of the faith. It was a time of confusion and tumult.

Things that were of great value in one age became useless in the next. All of the roles, structures, and relationships were focused on the new mission—getting the gospel out and converting the world to Jesus.

THE CHRISTENDOM PARADIGM

Beginning in the fourth century a new paradigm began to emerge.

The Church had to reinvent itself again. With the conversion of Constantine in 313 AD, he declared Christianity in name and in law to be the official religion of the empire. With this, your front door was no longer the mission field. Instead, the mission field was the political boundary of the empire—which was very far away. In order to reach the pagan world and incorporate it into the empire, and therefore Christianity, this was accomplished by military conquest. Think how this affected the Church and its mission.

Here are some points:

- The unity of the sacred and the secular: Bishops were now leaders in what we call "secular" things, such as raising and deploying armies and assuming major political roles, and kings and princes were leaders in what we call "religious things." It was Constantine himself who called the Council of Nicaea in 325 AD to define the faith against heresies and false doctrines of the day.

- The unity of the Church with the State to manage the empire: Administration, theology, and politics were all rolled up into one. There was only one church, and it was the empire. This is why heresy and treason were two sides of the same coin. The Church became institutionalized, and we have been working off that model for 1,500 years. In this model, to be a good citizen (Christian), one would be law-abiding, pay taxes, support religious and secular institutions, support efforts to enlarge the empire, be obedient to superiors, and support the whole system with your prayers and your life if need be. This describes America "to a tee" in the 1950s!

- So, one of the things that died out from the previous model was the personal engagement—the responsibility to witness and engage your culture for Christ. There was no need, the State/Church did that for you.

Consider this: most of the people who are leading churches today were trained under the Christendom Paradigm. The structures and institutions that make up the entire religious infrastructure of America are its mission societies and seminaries, congregational life, and religious books of order (discipline) are all taken off a newer revision model of the classical paradigm of the last 1,500 years. Even the Reformation did not change the model, just the theology. It has only been in the last fifty years or so that the Christendom Paradigm has come crashing down, and there is no clear model to replace it. Our society has been and still is in the process of becoming secularized.

There is no longer broad understanding of Christian principles or alignment with Christian institutions. In fact, it is quite the opposite, which is why, in part, prayer has been taken out of the schools, the Bible removed from public institutions, and "Under God" is waiting to be removed from the Pledge of Allegiance.

Our post-modern society is also post-Christian, and God is calling the Church to redefine and retool for a different world and a different mission—reinventing again. Now, we are in a world of space-age technology, the internet, and people groupings that are increasingly disconnected. In some ways, we have come full circle. The mission field again is outside our front door. The tragedy is that we are choosing to stay inside and watch Netflix.

As the Christendom model disintegrates, there is a real tension and confusion in pew land as well as in the house of the clergy. Roles are being redefined; mission is being redefined—it's almost like we are changing horses in midstream. The shells of the old structure are still all around us, even though many of them no longer work or hold any promise for the future. Some of these are institutions, some are roles, and some are mindsets.

We are at a critical inflection point, and our understanding of the prophetic calendar is essential as to how we approach the days ahead.

THREE FUNCTIONS OF GOD'S PEOPLE IN LAST DAYS MINISTRY

God's prophetic people are as F.F. Bruce says, "a hybrid people, born of the flesh in one age, but alive in the spirit in the age to come." Because the imprimatur of the Almighty is on us, we must engage in three functions to fulfill our supernatural destiny. They are seeing the invisible, hearing the inaudible, and doing the impossible. These three functions will distinguish an end-times people in the midst of an end-times harvest. Please join me in understanding these three critical functions.

1. Seeing the invisible. The Bible teaches us that the invisible realm is the more-important realm. Apostle Paul says in 2 Corinthians 4:18: "because we look not to the things that are seen but to the things that are unseen; for the things that are seen are transient, but the things that are unseen are eternal" (RSV). The challenge, however, is that although it's the more-important realm, it's not the more-immediate realm.

    We even see this in the natural order with what astronomer's call "dark matter." In the cosmos, the dark matter is much larger than the visible matter, (e.g. planets, asteroids, comets, etc.). Dark matter holds everything together; we just can't see it. I find this an amazing interface with New Testament truth. What does Paul say concerning Jesus in

Colossians: "… all things were created … through him and for him. He is before all things, and in him all things hold together."[197]

What if Joshua would have relinquished to only what he had seen: giants, walled cities, and vast fortifications?[198] There would not have been a land for Israel today. What if Elisha could not have seen the invisible protection of God when the armies of Ben-hadad surrounded the city where he dwelt?[199] What if Jesus would not have been able to see the resurrection and the outpouring of the Spirit at Pentecost. Could He have gone through Gethsemane and Calvary?[200] What if we fail to see the Church renewed in our day?[201] Seeing the invisible is realizing the will of God in any area of our lives. Paul had a revelation of his apostleship even though he was not one of the original twelve and went forth to conquer entire regions for the gospel.

The psalmist says, "To thee I lift up my eyes, O thou who art enthroned in the heavens!"[202] Jesus said the eye is the lamp of the body,[203] while the Psalmist says he will "behold wonderous things out of thy law" with his eyes.[204] Yes seeing is believing, especially the invisible.

2. Hearing the inaudible. The area of hearing is also linked to the concept of revelation. It will get us where we need to be. We are entering a time in history when our life depends on hearing what the Spirit is still saying to the churches. Just because it is inaudible does not mean that it is not discernable.

In the Old Testament, the tribe of Issachar was known for having an "understanding of the times." In fact, it was their weapon of choice. In the New Testament, Apostle John records that he was in the Spirit on the Lord's Day when he heard a loud voice like a trumpet instructing him to write on a scroll what he sees—and send it to seven churches. Here are some of the means of revelation:

- Direct revelation (Genesis 12:1–2)

- Dreams and visions (Daniel 7–8)

- The written Word (Exodus 20)

- Circumstances (John 6:37)

- Angels (Luke 2:10)

- -The Holy Spirit (Acts 16:6–7)

- The hearing ear and the seeing eye (Proverbs 20:12; Deuteronomy 4:10; Isaiah 1:2–3)

God has created a vehicle to receive revelation for which the history of Christianity is replete. The disciple John puts it plainly, "Truly, truly I say unto you, he who hears my word and believes him who sent me, has eternal life; he does not come into judgment, but has passed from death to life" (RSV).[205]

One day I was praying, and the Holy Spirit said, "Get up now and drive to Dayton (Ohio) and pray for your grand-father. He is about to die." My grandpa had been sick on many, many occasions but always recovered. However, the word was so specific, I gathered the family, and we left for his home. He also held a high ranking (thirty-third degree) in Freemasonry, and I knew I needed to present the gospel to him before he died.

We arrived at our destination two hours later, and immediately, I urged him to receive Christ as his only Savior. He did, and the next day he entered eternity. Friends, we must hear the inaudible. It can be a matter of life and death.

3. Doing the impossible. My exhortation here is that seeing the invisible and hearing the inaudible will position you to do the impossible. Revelation precedes actions for the seasoned Christian. In this, one will act like God, act for God, and act with God.

The King James Version on this verse is pressed into my memory: "(As it is written, 'I have made thee a father of many nations,) before him whom he believed, even God, who quickeneth the dead, and calleth those things which be not as though they were."[206]

There comes a time when we cease waiting on God, and God begins waiting on us. Remember these words: "For the eyes of the Lord run to and fro throughout the whole earth, to show his might in behalf of those whose heart is blameless toward him ...."[207] What we do with the revelation determines whether we do the impossible.[208]

Two final thoughts (points of emphasis) to summarize this section of the argument. First, we must discard the idea that doing the impossible is hard or difficult or unusual. Doing the miraculous is neither an effort nor unusual with God. In fact, it is the nature of God to reveal Himself, and that is what the miraculous is—a visible demonstration of the nature of God.

Watch others receive revelation when you act on the revelation you have. It is almost like a chain reaction.

Secondly, God desires to participate with us in the revelation of who He is. How else can one explain the incarnation? He did not want us to miss it. He still does not want us to miss it. Jesus is still the message, and when we begin to act as Jesus would act, even if it is offering a cup of cold water to a thirsty person, we will do what Jesus did.

The Scripture plainly says, "I tell you the truth, anyone who believes in me will do the same works I have done, and even greater works, because I am going to be with the Father."[209]

We must move in faith. Is the impossible hard for God? Of course not! It is not impossible either. The simple truth is God has given us a vehicle to move in the dimension He moves in; it is called faith.[210]

There you have it in a nutshell, the outworking of the Kingdom of God in your life and your world. What more is there than revelation and knowledge of God? Faith is acting on what you know. If you can walk in this, you can walk in God and do the impossible.

There comes a time to receive revelation, and there comes a time to walk in the revelation, and that time is now. The Apostle Paul says, "We are sons of light and sons of the day."[211]

Finally, the allegiance to one God and one God only caused a virulent prejudice against the Nation of Israel in the ancient world. That prejudice has carried itself all the way through to the present day. We are tasting some of what it has been like as Christianity intersects with the current culture of the United States.

The cancel culture crowd, the politically correct crowd, the anacronym crowd (Antifa and other antigovernment groups) hate the righteous standards of a Holy God. Yet we are called out of the nation of believers in Jesus, whatever our particular branding, to light the flame and keep it lit.[212]

In Israel of old, above all else, the flame was not to go out on the altar of the Lord. The whole nation corporately and the priests individually were keepers of the flame. The writer of Leviticus (Moses) mentions this three times inside of just a few verses. The emphasis is unmistakable. Our platform to approach a Holy God is the fire of His love and Word in our lives. We step into this ministry of the flame when we were transitioned from a formal priesthood in the Old Testament to a universal priesthood in the New Testament. The keepers of the flame of God's presence. Never, ever, let it go out. It becomes our priority, and our priorities determine our culture.

Work while it is day, for the night cometh when no man can work. Amen!

APPENDIX A

DEFENDING THE DECLARATION

ANYONE WHO IS WILLING TO DIG INTO original source material will soon realize the influence the Bible and Christianity had upon the Founding Fathers and our Founding documents. My purpose in this appendix is a follow-up and expansion of chapter six, "The Government of God in the Earth," while attempting to set the record straight concerning the origin of the Declaration of Independence as a document that spawned the greatest human governmental experiment in the history of mankind.

To do this, I have relied heavily on the author and historian Gary Amos. He spent close to ten years studying original source material used to justify the Declaration and four years to write a refutation of the party-line narrative that the Declaration is a secular document. It had its roots in Enlightenment rationality while being transported by the vehicle of deism, particularly resident in John Locke (1632–1704) and other seventeenth- and eighteenth-century Enlightenment philosophers. Unfortunately, this version of the Declaration has been taunted by secular and Christian authors of note and is the predominate view being taught in most colleges and universities across the nation.

Mr. Amos has secured degrees in jurisprudence and theology, precisely because he maintains that the Declaration of Independence is a legal document of theological significance. It has its roots in "the Bible, Christian theology, the Western Christian intellectual tradition, and medieval Christianity."[213] His book, *Defending the Declaration*, has become a kind of debater's manual for defending the influence of Christianity on the Declaration. It has completely upended the narrative that the Declaration was a product of secular, rational, anti- Christian Enlightenment thinking. In fact, it is just the opposite with the prevailing myth beginning to crumble as we enter the twenty-first century.

As we launch into this discussion, we will pull some of the key concepts in the Declaration and hold them up to historical analysis, discerning their true origin found at least 700 years prior to the creation of the Declaration. Even with this, we can only skim the surface but hopefully ignite an interest for further study for those so inclined.

WHAT IS DEISM?

Deism is a worldview which maintains that if God was the Creator of the universe, then He "after setting it in motion abandoned it, assumed no control over life, exerted no influence on natural phenomena, and gave no supernatural revelation."[214] Apparently, this God is a kind of watchmaker God, an absentee God phenomenon. This is, of course, in opposition to what the Bible reveals about God as actively involved in running His world and revealing Himself to mankind.

Deism takes a sharp right turn, conceiving God as "exerting his power and revealing his will indirectly through his creation rather than directly through miraculous manifestation and the Bible."[215]

The historian Carl Becker wrote a very convincing book in 1922, popularizing the deistic fable behind the American Revolution. He stated that "nature had stepped in between man and God; so that there was no longer any way to know God's will except by discovering the 'laws' of Nature, which would doubtless be the laws of 'nature's' god as Jefferson said."[216] Basically, Becker was saying that deism gave birth to John Locke's ideas about God and the nature of the world and that through Locke, Thomas Jefferson gave birth to the American Revolution.

However, as we skim the landscape of history and look at some of the key phrases in the Declaration, we will establish that they were popularized 500 years before the Declaration of Independence.

THE LAW OF NATURE AND NATURE'S GOD

The terms "law of nature" and the "law of God" were part of Christian legal and theological language at least 500 years before the rise of deism and 700 years before the American Revolution. A study of English common law will reveal the same. The two terms were used as part of Catholic theology and common law as early as the eleventh century. They were used during the Protestant Reformation, particularly on the Reformed side with John Calvin and the Puritans. In addition, the concepts were a part of English common law and stated in documents from the Magna Carta (1215) to the English Bill of Rights (1689).[217] Furthermore, John Locke used these terms without changing their meaning.

So, what do they mean?

In the span of 500 years before John Locke, the term "law of nature" stood for the eternal moral law of God stamped in the creation and inscribed on the conscience of men's hearts. The term the "law of God" meant the same eternal moral law, only as revealed supernaturally in the Old and New Testaments. These terms are a kind of shorthand way to express a very broad set of ideas and principles. The entire colonial jurisprudence system was based on these laws of right and wrong, good and evil. These terms were common in English common law and were underwritten and understood in the colonial charters.

The Christian tradition spoke of the "laws of nature and the laws of God" as two sides of the same coin based partly upon the Apostle Paul's discourse in Romans 1 and 2, especially Romans 1:18ff. In the Old Testament, the general revelation of God's moral law to all men is scene throughout the book of Job and in Psalm 19 where God uses creation as a teaching tool to communicate His ordinances among men. These and many other passages speak of a moral law revealed in nature or creation which men cannot escape. In Genesis 8:22, Moses records, "While the earth remains, seedtime and harvest, cold and heat, summer and winter, day and night, shall not cease."[218] These precepts in theology are called "general revelation."

John Locke referenced the Scriptures in explaining political principles. His essay on Human Understanding (1690) openly states that the Bible is a special divine revelation of the highest authority from God to man. Listen to what Locke says about the Bible and supernatural revelation:

> The holy Scripture is to me, and always will be, the constant guide of my belief; and I shall always harken to it,

as containing infallible truth relating to things of the highest concernment. And I wish I could say there are no mysteries int it; I acknowledge there are to me, and I fear always will be. But where I lack the evidence of things, there yet is ground enough for me to believe, because God has said it: and I shall immediately condemn and quit any opinion of mine, as soon as I am shown that it is contrary to any revelation in the holy scripture.[219]

"So heavily did Locke draw from the Bible in developing his political theories that in his first treatise on government (Two Treatises of Government 1690), he invoked the Bible in 1,349 times; in his second treatise, he cited it 157 times.[220] After all, Locke was considered to be a theologian with two major writings of religious significance to his credit.[221] He admitted that everything in the Old and New Testaments were "infallibly true," since it was the will of God clothed in words.[222] He stated in several of his works that both nature and Scripture were declarations of God's eternal law. When one pairs this with William Blackstone (1723–1780), the greatest legal mind of the Colonial Era, who also parroted similar themes in his writings, one comes away with a clear dependence on divine revelation in the affairs of man guiding them in the most sacred truths concerning the world we live in. William Blackstone was required reading at most colonial universities. "His Commentaries on the Laws, introduced in 1766, became the law book of the Founding Fathers."[223]

John Adams, the second president of the United States, was on the draft committee with Thomas Jefferson and linked the "law of nature" with Galatians 5:14 and Matthew 7:2. Earlier in life, Adams was actually preparing for a ministerial career but was sidetracked by a Worcester lawyer, yet retaining his bent toward the Christian faith and divine revelation. On one occasion, he said, "One great Advantage of the Christian Religion is that it brings the great Principle of the Law of Nature and Nations, Love your Neighbor as yourself, and do to others as you would that others would do to you,—to the Knowledge, Belief and Veneration of the whole People."[224]

SELF-EVIDENT TRUTHS

The Declaration of Independence says, "We hold these truths to be self-evident...", which is "so clear and obvious to the ordinary person that they require no proof"[225] while basing the Declaration on a theory of knowledge which professional philosophers call epistemology. As Gary Amos says in his book *Defending the Declaration*, "Ironically, the term "'self-evident,' more than all the others discussed in this book, is the one that most clearly shows the impact of Christianity on the Declaration."[226] Here we are talking about "intuitive knowledge," which means it is in you by virtue of your creator.

Something is self-evident to us when we are innately or naturally aware of it. For example, when a man looks at a woman, he is innately aware that she is different than he is at several significant points. This is precisely why when Adam saw Eve in Genesis 2:23, he said, "this now at last!" (exclamation added).

The term self-evident came into common use in the late 1500s. Translating the Latin "per se notum," i.e., nature is "to know" while "per se" is "through the agency of our own efforts or self."[227] The Enlightenment rationalists did not coin the term. Medieval theologians used it centuries earlier including St. John of

Damascus (749 A.D.). St. Thomas Aquinas, 400 years before John Locke, spoke of it as "the precepts, therefore contained in the Decalogue are those the knowledge of which man has in himself from God."[228] The words "phaneros en autois" (evident in themselves) taken from Romans 1:19 are the biblical counterpart to the Latin "per se notum" or self-evident.[229]

Thomas Jefferson was saying that certain truths are self- evident that have been stamped on man's conscience from the creation and are therefore intuitive because they came to him as a mark of God's image. This is then consistent with Christianity, which teaches "that man's rationality is the first dimension of Godlikeness and the basis for all other dimensions of Godlikeness."[230]

In addition, "the New Testament uses about forty different Greek words to convey its message about the mind. Words dealing with the reason, mind, and intellect occur more than 1,500 times in the New Testament."[231]

To claim that reason, rationality and the mind are products of Enlightenment thinking when considering the natural world is preposterous. God gave us these faculties to negotiate a cultural environment with "enlightened" understanding. For this, we should be grateful.

UNALIENABLE RIGHTS

"America was founded on 'unalienable rights'—those that a man may not unconditionally sell, trade, barter, or transfer without denying the image of God in himself. God the creator endows man with these rights, annexing them to the human race. They are inalienable. For to deny these rights in a man is to deny that he is a human being."[232]

Because of Christianity's emphasis on the supreme importance and value of each person, this area of inalienable rights is traced almost exclusively to biblical ideas, much to the chagrin of the humanists. The word for "rights" in the Old Testament is mishpat and occurs over 400 times. The concepts of justice and right are interlocked throughout the Old Testament. We are talking about rightly ordered relationships and a moral order imposed on those relationships. God asks the question to Abraham in a hotly contested dispute: "… Shall not the Judge of all the earth do right."[233]

In Deuteronomy 1:17 (NLT), the Lord God instructs those who are assisting Moses in the administration of justice to "be impartial in your judgments. Hear the cases of those who are poor as well as those who are rich. Don't be afraid of anyone's anger, for the decision you make is God's decision …." God is the source of all authority, rights, and justice. Western civilization has and still does base its legal structure on these concepts. The word mishpat is translated "cause" or legal case in many verses including Numbers 27:5.[234] In addition, it is translated as a "right" in Deuteronomy 21:17.[235]

Gary Amos sums it up nicely:

The Biblical uses of the word *mishpat* can be divided therefore into two broad meanings. First, *mishpat* is justice: an objectively ordered relationship between God and man, and between men and men, including a body of legal and moral precepts and the right order itself. Second, *mishpat* is a subjective personal right inherent in one's being, part of what it means to be a person since man is created in God's image. Thus, the Bible provides for an objectively revealed moral law from which flow objectively ordered relationships and for individual rights.[236]

From the above understanding, we can see that the concepts of "life, liberty, and the pursuit of happiness" set in the Declaration of Independence is a state of existence that comes from obeying the laws of the creator and the creation. Right living lends itself to a substantial state of happiness that the New Testament calls a state of "blessed."[237] When our living is right living in God's eyes, as when man pleases God, then one's life is blessed and bends toward real happiness.

However, the opposite is true; when one's actions are displeasing to the Lord. They become "destructive" and translate into a state of unhappiness. All of these concepts were part of English common law and known well by the revolution of 1776.

GOVERNMENT BY THE CONSENT OF THE GOVERNED

The bulk of contemporary writing on the American Revolution in 1776 would lend the average person to believe that the colonies were rebels against God and the king of England. This, in turn, has caused many Christians to be ashamed of the American founding and defensive about its origins. The fact is, however, the Declaration of Independence is not about revolution but instead about lawfully changing a form of government when the present government becomes tyrannical and despotic. The document actually states these reasons and encompasses two-thirds of the entire text with a "history of repeated injuries and usurpations." As Gary Amos explains, this Declaration amounts to a "complete turn of a wheel in a backwards direction, to restore a previous order or balance."[238]

The Declaration of Independence bases itself on the compact theory of government because the relationship between England and the colonies was based on a compact of covenant. The essence of the compact were certain promises between the king and the colonists. He would rule, and they would cooperate as long as he fulfilled the conditions of the compact. The word "compact" is equivalent to the Latin "pactum" translated in the Hebrew Old Testament as "berith" or covenant. A tyranny was experienced opening the colonists to the Christian theory of lawful revolution.

Taxation with representation was one of the items in dispute. At such a point, the people have a right of self-defense and are freed from any further obligation under the agreement. The compact or covenant was a formal agreement between two parties, sworn by an oath, and ratified by a public ceremony. By the time, of the revolution, dozens of abridgments were cited in the Declaration to substantiate a break with England.

In the event of such a breach of compact, "lower officers who still have a right to rule can declare a change of government."[239] The people can restrict tyrants only through lawful representation. This is part of the theory of revolution known as "interposition."[240] Those who have remained faithful to the law, interpose themselves between a despotic higher ruler and the people who are oppressed. There is clear biblical precedent for this found in 2 Chronicles 22. When Queen Athaliah, mother of King Ahaziah, declared herself queen of Israel, she did so while trying to kill all the royal line of Judah after her son died.[241] Only the infant Joash survived, because he was hidden by the priest Jehoiada, only later to be enthroned as the rightful ruler later in a public ceremony.[242]

The colonial rulers in America were not "humanists" rebels who decided to determine their own fate because they tired of English rule. Under the law of nature and nature's God, these people had a right to throw off the well-documented tyranny of King George lll of England. They believed God saw them through even though they were pathetically outmanned and outgunned, having to face the greatest naval fleet in the world at the time.

Their conclusion to these events can be seen in the final paragraph of the Declaration of Independence:

> We, therefore, the representatives of the UNITED STATES OF AMERICA, in General Congress assembled, appealing to the Supreme Judge of the world for the rectitude of our intentions, do, in the name, and by the authority for the good people of these colonies, solemnly publish and declare That these United Colonies are, and of right ought to" be, FREE and INDEPENDENT STATES; that they are absolved from all allegiance, to the British crown, and that all political connexion between them and the state of Great Britain is, and ought to be, totally dissolved; and that, as FREE and INDEPENDENT STATES, they have full power to levy war, conclude peace, contract alliances, establish commerce, and to do all other acts and things which INDEPENDENT STATES may of right do.
>
> And for the support of this Declaration, with a firm reliance on the protection of DIVINE PROVIDENCE, we mutually pledge to each other our lives, our fortunes, and our sacred honour.[243]

CONCLUSION

Mr. Amos sums up nicely the import of the revolution and the document that give it birth:

> The American Revolution, as enshrined in the terms of the Declaration of Independence, was both legal and Christian. It was legal in that it was carried out on principles which had been part and parcel of the British law tradition for centuries. It was "Christian" in that all the principles included in the Declaration of Independence agreed with, and probably grew directly from, the Biblical teaching about revolution as formulated by major Catholic and Protestant theorists over a span of seven hundred years.[244]

Finally, it should be stated that many Christian historians believe that the ideas in the Declaration were not Christian even if many of the colonists were. However, there is a growing number of authors who believe that the ideas in the Declaration were Christian, even if some of the founders were not. Our hope is that those who care enough to research the founding of our Republic will, as Abraham Lincoln said in the Gettysburg Address, experience a "new birth of freedom" even in the troubled days of the twenty-first century in America.

The time is now!

APPENDIX B

HOW TO MAINTAIN HUNGER FOR GOD IN A SELF-INDULGENT MATERIALISTIC CULTURE: AN EXHORTATION TO THE BODY OF CHRIST

MANY TODAY ARE FOUND RAVAGED in the House of God by the prevailing winds of secular society. They feel smothered by the constant refrain of "political correctness" or "cancel culture" or the worldwide pandemic known as COVID-19. At the same time, the Church seems to give a desperate message in the face of overcoming odds.

We are not the first generation to feel the "squeeze" of a godless environment; however, we may be the last. In such times, our only refuge is in the Word of God. The sure and certain Word of the Bible has held the believing community throughout history, and it is not about to stop now. Perhaps you feel beleaguered, worn down, and exhausted by the present world system. The Apostle Paul tell us that "... creation itself will be set free from its bondage to decay"[245] (Romans 8:21), so take heart. The prophets of old still deliver good news to a waiting world. They encouraged Jesus and they still can deliver the goods to us as well.

What you are about to read is not meant to be a formula, but instead a kind of roadmap. With a roadmap, you have to do the driving, but you will arrive if you stay on course while being assured of your final destination as you journey down the road. Just keep looking at the map and your current mile marker.

In this case, our map is leading to "maintaining hunger for God in a materialistic culture." I find this to be one of the great challenging issues in the Church today. How does the average person "stay current" with God when surrounded by the wealth and affluence of American life? We have so much of everything that our life context becomes smothered by the materialism that engulfs us on a daily basis. If we are going to swim away from this "undertow," we have to become more focused and intentional about our walk with God.

We begin with Jeremiah 29:12–13: "Then you will call upon me and come and pray to me, and I will hear you. You will seek me and find me; when you seek me with all your heart." In this Scripture, Jeremiah is encouraging the Jewish captives who have been displaced from their homes and their homeland and find themselves in a totally foreign environment while having to adapt to a new way of life. His promise comes with a caveat. Christian history is filled with folks who have taken Him at His Word and have come out on the other end on fire for God.

John Piper, a popular author, has written a well-published workbook on this subject. Presently, America could be the most difficult nation in the world to do this; but do it we shall. Another ancient prophet who enjoins a similar refrain is Isaiah of Jerusalem. Eight hundred years before Christ, he said, "Then you shall call,

and the Lord will answer; you shall cry, and he will say, Here I am
…."[246] I could fill out the page with similar exhortations from the
Bible, but the point is, God is waiting for us to call upon Him in
the hour of our need.

From this perch, I desire to share four areas of engagement
which could lead the interested believer to greater heights of hunger for God in the midst of our current cultural chaos in America.

First, stay in the Word. Jesus tells us in Rev.3:20; "Behold, I
stand at the door and knock; if any one hears my voice and opens
the door, I will come in to him and eat with him, and he with me."
I don't know about you, but I find this to be a direct invitation from
the King of Kings for fellowship and communion. Anyone familiar
with sitting down and eating a meal in the Middle Eastern fashion
knows this to be an engaging, intimate time of conversation and
friendship. This invitation from Jesus is ongoing throughout our
spiritual journey in this world.

A famous artist in 1851, painted a picture of Jesus standing
at the door of a vine-covered cottage, knocking on the front door.
The artist's name was Holman Hunt. Perhaps you have seen this
painting. If one looks closely, the door has no handle on the outside. It must be opened by those on the inside. Friends, this is a
standing invitation from Jesus to open the door or our hearts and
let Him in.

Another penetrating Scripture in this vein is found in the
Song of Solomon 5:3. In this passage, a woman's beloved is knocking at her chamber door, but the maiden resists getting up to answer because "I have taken off my robe—must I put it on again?
I have washed my feet—must I soil them again?" (NIV). She is
in a state of "repose," her comfort is more important to her than
her relationship with her beloved! I believe this to be a picture of

the Church in America. Our comfort culture is eating us from the inside out. The invisible bonds of materialism have lulled us into repose, like marijuana, the gateway drug leading millions into a physical repose—deadening their world.

Someone had said, "Marijuana is the host that seats you at the table of addiction." In addition, when the call of God beckons, if we hesitate because we are busy, distracted, or lazy like this woman in SOS 5, just a few minutes later can make all the difference in the world, and we miss the thing at the door. What is knocking at the door of your life right now—opportunity, mission, education, financial stewardship, mentoring?

Hunger is an active state; it results in your seeking out the object of desire that will satisfy your need. You are probably reading this book today because of some sense of hunger for God. But to get to hunger, one has to distance themselves from that object of desire.

There is a price to pay. We must plant the seed before we see the crop.

Secondly, pray and fast. *Roses Book of Bible Charts, Maps, and Time Lines* designate 100 prayers taken from thirty-five books of the Bible. Obviously, prayer is foundational to any relationship with God. The more we pray, the closer we get. The less we pray, the father we drift. Philippians 4:6 is a key word on prayer: "Have no anxiety about anything, but in everything by prayer and supplication with thanksgiving let your requests be made known to God."

Following their exile to the nations of the world, God said, "Then you will call upon me and come and pray to me, and I will hear you." We began with the Scripture from Jeremiah 29:12. However, reading further into Jeremiah 29:14, He said, "... I will bring you back to the place from which I sent you into exile." They did seek His face, and He did bring them back home again. Prayer is absolutely vital in this process of maintaining hunger for God.

As far as fasting is concerned, it has not been widely practiced through the history of the Church. In America, more fasting is practiced relative to dieting than to spirituality. There are many good resources on fasting available to the Church today. I recommend the author Jensen Franklin. The prophet Joel gave us a timely exhortation to fast in chapter 1:14–15: "Sanctify a fast, call a solemn assembly. Gather the elders and all the inhabitants of the land to the house of the Lord your God; and cry to the Lord. Alas for the day! For the day of the Lord is near, and as destruction from the Almighty it comes."

In light of our emphasis throughout this book on the end times, this gets particularly close. Joel's description is forceful with a local invasion coming on the land of Israel, foreshadowing a day of judgment for Judah as well as judgment connected to the day of the Lord.

There are times that require simple fasting to be added to one's devotion to God. I believe today is one of those days in America. In addition, when Jesus drove demons out of a boy who was deaf and dumb in Mark 9, His disciples asked Him why they couldn't do it. He replied "This kind cannot be driven out by anything but prayer and fasting."[247] If you have not already, I encourage you to add fasting to your personal walk with God. It will do wonders for your spiritual awareness.

Thirdly, join an affinity group. In 1729, John Wesley joined a small group of students who desired to live out a vital Christianity in a group called the Holy Club. They were taunted by fellow students with demeaning nicknames: Reforming Club, Godly Club,

Sacramentarians, Bible Moths, Bible Bigots, and Supererogation Men. But the one that stuck was Methodist. They met on Sunday evenings, they read the Greek New Testament and the classics; fasted on Wednesdays and Fridays; received the Lord's Supper every week; visited the poor and imprisoned, including those on death row, and brought all their life under review. Wesley said, "I began not only to read but study the Bible as the one and only standard of truth and the model of pure religion."[248] (History is replete with folks who have done this and succeeded. It works!

That group included his brother Charles Wesley who wrote some 6,000 hymns; George Whitfield, who spawned the Great Awakening in America; Mr. Hervey, a publisher in Leeds, England and author of *Meditations Among the Tombs*; Mr. John Clayton, afterwards chaplain of the Collegiate Church of Manchester: Mr. Benjamin Ingram, known as the Yorkshire evangelist; Mr. Thomas Broughton, afterwards secretary of S.P.C.K. (the Society for the Promotion of Christian Knowledge);[249] Robert Kirkham, the brother of Wesley's first sweetheart; Mr. William Morgan, the son of an Irish gentleman; and Mr. John Gambold, who afterwards became a Moravian bishop.[250] God uses those who yield! Becoming a part of an affinity group will cover fellowship, encouragement, accountability, and discipleship, the central and final command of Jesus.[251] Christianity is meant to be lived out in community.[252]

Finally, The baptism in the Holy Spirit. In 1960, Dennis Bennett, an Episcopal priest from Van Nuys, California, was baptized in the Holy Spirit and spoke in tongues. That flame ignited a fire in the entire denominational world in America known as the Charismatic renewal. I lead a group of international leaders today that was started by Dennis Bennett in 1970. At a spiritual life retreat for students at Duquesne University in 1967, it jumped over and inflamed the entire Catholic world. Today there are some 650 million Spirit-baptized Christians in the world.

The Church has accumulated tons of research and libraries of books on the subject. It has become the first truly worldwide revival in history encompassing not only the Protestant world but the Catholic world, the Orthodox Church, and the Messianic Jewish believers. One of the spin-offs of this move of God has been a broad pursuit of unity in the Body of Christ. I recently did a major teaching on unity and its antecedents as we entered the year 2020. If you are not pursuing unity in the Body of Christ today, you are in danger of becoming a lone ranger.

These four simple guidelines will ensure the awareness of your inheritance in Christ as you navigate the current culture in America. I preached a message years ago that helped many to encapsulate "a sure path" to victory in their daily walk with God. It is called "How to Withdraw from the Bank of Heaven." Perhaps it will help you as well.

HOW TO WITHDRAW FROM THE BANK OF HEAVEN

1. **Decide** (Job 22:28)" "you will decide on a matter and it will be established for you, and light will shine on your ways." (Under the unction of the Holy Spirit, decide upon what the Lord is saying to you now.)

2. **Agree** (Matthew 18:19): "Again I say to you, if two of you agree on earth about anything they ask, it will be done for them by my Father who is in heaven." (God loves like-mindedness—unity, e.g. the Trinity)

3. **Lay Hold of It** (Mark 11:24): "Therefore I tell you, whatever you ask in prayer, believe that you have received it, and it will be yours." (1 Timothy 6:9: "Lay hold of the life that is life indeed.") Some things are given to us in this life. Draw them to yourself.

4. **Bind the Rat** (Matthew 18:18) "Truly I say unto you, whatever you bind on earth shall be bound in heaven, and whatever you loose on earth shall be loosed in heaven." (Authority to administrate the Kingdom.)

5. **Loose the Ministering Spirits** (Hebrews 1:14): "Are they not all ministering spirits sent forth to serve, for the sake of those who are to obtain salvation?" (Gr. Diaconis=servants of us.) God has assigned an angel to your path in life.

6. **Praise God for It** (Philippians 4:6–7): "Have no anxiety about anything, but in everything by prayer and supplication with thanksgiving let your requests be made known to God. And the God of peace will keep your hearts and minds in Christ Jesus."

Conclusion: Remember, with a roadmap, you have to do the driving.

BOOKS PUBLISHED BY SCOTT T. KELSO

The Truth About Grace (Charisma/E-21, 2018)

Biblical Eldership: Back to the Future with Spirit Filled Leadership in the Local Church (Word & Spirit Press, 2016)

Let's See What Sticks: Kingdom Living in Chaotic Times (WinePress Publishers, 2013: Trusted Books, 2014, Second Edition)

Ice on Fire: A New Day for the 21st Century Church (Thomas Nelson Publishers), 2006

ABOUT THE AUTHOR

SCOTT T. KELSO

SCOTT KELSO ministers in the areas of teaching, preaching, healing and writing, and has a long history of ministering to pastors and their spouses. His deep passion for evangelism and outreach has given him a heart for missions, and Scott has been on missions to Africa, Israel, the Philippines, Mexico, Cuba, and Brazil.

He is a past president of Aldersgate Renewal Ministries in Goodlettsville, Tennessee, and currently serves on the advisory council. Scott also serves as President of the Charismatic Leaders Fellowship, an international group of top-tier leaders from all five streams of Christianity (Catholic, Orthodox, Protestant, nondenominational, and Pentecostal) pursuing unity in the Body of Christ. He has been elected to the Jurisdictional and General Conference of the United Methodist Church several times. Scott is the author of *Ice on Fire: A New Day for the 21ˢᵗ Century Church* published by Thomas Nelson.

Scott earned his Doctor of Ministry degree from the United Theological Seminary in Dayton, Ohio, in Supernatural Ministry with the Randy Clark Scholars in 2015. He and his wife Linda live in Pataskala, Ohio. They have three children and seven grandchildren.

FivePoints-GCAN.org
CharismaticLeadersFellowship.org

ENDNOTES

1. God's heart has always been to walk with a committed people. One can observe this pattern well into the history of Israel with Yahweh. Consider Is.48:17: "This is what the Lord says—your Redeemer, the Holy One of Israel: 'I am the Lord your God, who teaches you what is good for you and leads you along the paths you should follow'" (NLT). Scripture references throughout will be from the New Living Translation of the Bible unless otherwise noted.

2. Charles J. Chaput, *Strangers in a Strange Land: Living the Catholic Faith in a Post-Christian World*, (New York: Henry Holt and Company, 2017), 44.

3. Charles Spurgeon, *The Treasury of David, Vol.2, Psalm 138*, (Byron Center, MI: Associated Publishers & Authors, 1970), 204.

4. Richard Elliott Friedman, *The Bible with Sources Revealed: A New View into the Five Books of Moses* (New York, NY: HarperOne, An Imprint of Harper Collins Publishers, 2003), 3-5.

5. Winfried Corduan, *In the Beginning God: A Fresh Look at the Case for Original Monotheism* (Nashville, Tn: B&H Publishing Group, 2013), 341.

6. Ibid., 344.

7. Ibid., 342.

8. Donald E. Miller, *Reinventing American Protestantism: Christianity in the New Millennium* (Berkeley/Los Angeles/London: University of California Press, 1997), 6.

9. Ibid., 7.

10. Ibid.

11. Brandon Hatmaker, *A Mile Wide: Trading a Shallow Religion for a Deeper Faith* (Nashville, TN: Nelson Books, An Imprint of Thomas Nelson, 2016), xiii. The phrase comes from a 1889 American journalist and humorist, Edgar Nye, who introduced the phrase when referring to a real river called the Platte River in the western United States. It remains to this day an important tributary system in the Missouri River watershed, however disqualified from use because of its lack of depth.

12. Ibid, xiv.

13. George R. Hunsberger and Craig Van Gelder, ed., *The Church Between Gospel and Culture* (Grand Rapids, MI: William B. Eerdmans Publishing Company, 1996), 34–35.

14. By taking this approach, they too, along with the modernists/rationalists, utilize a rationalistic paradigm to interpret the Bible.

15. In today's context, I refer to visitors as "seeker silhouettes" because in many cases, they are there but not really. A silhouette is an outline of a person or thing lacking definition and true recognition. Giving the appearance of self-decency, they are there to observe, not commit.

16. Frederic C. Putnam, Ph.D. *The Complete Biblical Library: Proverbs, Ecclesiastics, Song of Songs* (Springfield, MO: World Library Press, Inc. 1990), 207.

17. See Ex. 20:13; 21:22; 23:7; Lev. 18:21; Deut. 24:16; Prov. 6:16–17, 15:3.

18. Matt. 19:4.

19. https://churchleaders.com/news/383605-george-barna-another-reformation.html (Referenced 20Oct.2020)

20. A.W. Tozer, *I Talked Back to the Devil: The Fighting Fervor of the Victorious Christian*, (Camp Hills, PA: Wingspread Publishers, 2001).

21. Robert S. Elwood, *The Sixties Spiritual Awakening: American Religion Moving for Modern to Postmodern* (New Brunswick, NJ: Rutgers University Press, 1994), 249.

22. Robert H. Bork, *Slouching Towards Gomorrah: Modern Liberalism and American Decline* (New York, NY: Regan Books, 1996).

23. Ibid. 51.

24. Ross Douthat, *Bad Religion: How We Became A Nation of Heretics* (New York, NY: Free Press, 2012), 63.

25. Ibid.

26. Roger Kimball, *The Long March: How the Cultural Revolution of the 1960s Changed America* (New York, NY: Encounter Books, 2000), 34.

27. Gertrude Himmelfarb, *One Nation, Two Cultures* (New York, NY: Alfred A. Knopf, 1999), 16.

28. Michael Anton, *The Stakes: America at the Point of No Return* (Washington, DC: Regnery Publishing, 2020), 97.

29. Ibid. xi.

30. Ibid. Jacket.

31. *The Sixties Spiritual Awakening*, p.261.

32. Ibid. 261.

33. *Slouching*, p.51.

34. Francis Fukuyama, *The Great Disruption: Human Nature and the Reconstitution of Social Order* (New York, NY: The Free Press, 1999), 13.

35. Sean Hannity, *Live Free or Die: America (and the world) On the Brink* (New York, NY: Threshold Editions, 2020), 20.

36. Ibid. 21.

37. Ibid. 21.

38. Ibid.

39. Ibid. 23.

40. Ibid. 24.

41. *The Stakes*, 98.

42. Ibid., 98.

43. Ibid., 99.

44. Ibid., 99.

45. Ibid., 101.

46. Ibid., 102.

47. Chilton Williamson Jr., *After Tocqueville: The Promise and Failure of Democracy* (Wilmington, DE: ISI Books, 2012), 1.

48. Ibid.

49. Alexis de Tocqueville, *Democracy in America, Vol.1,* (New Rochelle, NY: Arlington House), 298.

50. Ibid.

51. Ibid. 299.

52. Ibid. 294.

53. Ibid. 296.

54. *After de Tocqueville*, 67

55. *Democracy in America*, 297.

56. Charles J. Chaput, *Strangers in a Strange Land: Living the Catholic Faith in a Post-Christian World* (New York, NY: Henry Holt and Company, 2017), 5.

57. Cal Thomas, *America's Expiration Date: The Fall of Empires and Super-powers and the Future of the United States*, (Grand Rapids, MI: Zondervan Books, 2020), 18.

58. *Strangers*, p.110.

59. James M. Kushiner, ed., *Creed & Culture* (Wilmington, DE: ISI Books, 2003), 3.

60. Jake Meador, *In Search of the Common Good: Christian Fidelity in a Fractured World* (Downers Grove, IL: IVP Books, 2019), 31.

61. Pastor James Dewhurst: Real Church, Pataskala, Ohio; 9 August, 2020.

62. Fox News Alert, 22 August, 2020, Robert Gearty, reporting.

63. See Lev. 10:10; 1 Ki. 3:19; Prov. 16:21; Is. 58:8–9; Jn. 7:24; Ro. 12:1–2; 2 Cor. 10:4–5; Phil. 1:9–10; Heb. 5:11–14.

64. Jay E. Adams, *A Call to Discernment: Distinguishing Truth from Error in Today's Church* (Eugene, OR: Harvest House Publishers, 1987), 32.

65. See Judges 21:25.

66. *A Call*, p.49.

67. Timothy M. Gallagher, O.M.V., *The Discernment of Spirits: An Ignatian Guide for Everyday Living* (New York, NY: Crossroad Publishing Company, 2005), 15.

68. Ibid., 17.

69. Ibid., 30.

70. Ibid., 29.

71. Ibid., 31.

72. William Byron Forbush, D.D.ed., *Fox's Book of Martyrs* (Grand Rapids, MI: Zondervan Publishing House, 1981), 9.

73. Wikipedia

74. *A Call*, p. 46.

75. Steven Garofalo, *Right for You but Not for Me: A Response to Moral Relativism* (Charlotte, NC: Triedstone Publishing Company, 2013), 82.

76. Ibid.

77. Alister E. McGrath, *Mere Discipleship: Growing in Wisdom and Hope* (Grand Rapids, MI: Baker Books, 2018), 43.

78. Ibid.

79. David Watson, *Called and Committed: World-Changing Discipleship* (Wheaton, Il: Harold Shaw Publishers, 1982), 110.

80. A clear example can be found in Jer. 7:1–11.

81. Ibid.

82. Ibid.

83. Ibid., 112.

84. Shawn Bolz, *Translating God: Hearing God's Voice for Yourself and the World Around You* (Glendale, CA: ICreate Productions, 2015), 72.

85. Shawn Bolz, *Translating God*, p.18.

86. Ibid. 18.

87. Ibid. 20.

88. Scott Kelso, *Let's See What Sticks: Kingdom Living in Chaotic Times* (Enumclaw, WA, 2013), 98.

89. Shawn Bolz, *Translating God*, p.99.

90. Kim Clement, *Call Me Crazy but I'm Hearing God: Secrets to Hearing the Voice of God* (Shippensburg, PA: Destiny Image Publishers, Inc. 2007), 14.

91. *Let's See*, p. 98.

92. Laurence W. Wood, *The Meaning of Pentecost in Early Methodism* (Lanham, Maryland & Oxford, 2002),

93. *Let's See*, p. 102.

94. Ibid., p. 103.

95. The Reverend Everett L. Fullam: *Paul, People, and Prayer*, St. Paul's Episcopal Church, (Darien, CT).

96. Shawn Bolz, *Translating God*, p.60.

97. James W. Goll, *The Seer: The Prophetic Power of Visions, Dreams, and Open Heavens [Expanded Edition]* (Shippensburg, PA: Destiny Image Publishers, Inc. 2012), 28.

98. Shawn Bolz, *Translating God*, p.143.

99. Michael Sullivant, *Prophetic Etiquette* (Lake Mary, FL: Creation House, 2000), 204.

100. Jon Mark Ruthven, *What's Wrong with Protestant Theology: Tradition vs. Biblical Emphasis* (Tulsa, OK: Word & Spirit Press, 2013), 24-25.

101. Kim Clement, *Call Me Crazy*, 194.

102. Ibid.

103. Jon Mark Ruthven, *What's Wrong with Protestant Theology*, 1.

104. Ibid., 35.

105. Rev. 11:15.

106. Rev. 12:11.

107. See Ex. 15:11; Dt. 3:24; 4:7; Micah 7:18–19; Ps. 113: 505.

108. Gerhard Von Rad, *God at Work in Israel* (Nashville, TN: Abingdon Press, 1980), 91.

109. 1 Cor.4:1.

110. See Is. 44:14–17.

111. Josh. 24:19–28.

112. Ecc. 12:13–14 RSV.

113. Institute in Basic Youth Conflicts

114. Lk. 8:17 RSV.

115. Lk. 12:3 RSV.

116. Ps. 94:9 RSV.

117. Prov. 5:21. See also Prov. 15:3 RSV.

118. See Is. 50:10 and 51:7, 12.

119. Zondervan Pictorial Encyclopedia of the Bible, p.518.

120. Ibid.

121. Gen. 28:16–17 RSV.

122. Deut. 6:4–5 RSV.

123. Prov. 1:7; 2:6; 9:10; 15:33; 22:4; 24:14.

124. Mal. 3:16–18 RSV.

125. Ecc. 1:9 NLT.

126. Judg. 21: 25.RSV.

127. Gen. 2:16–17 RSV. Compare 1 John 2:15–16.

128. Mk. 1:15 RSV.

129. Gen. 2:19.

130. Gen. 1:28.

131. J.I. Packer, *Seeing God in the Dark: Unraveling the Mysteries of Holy Living* (Peabody, MA: Hendrickson Publishers, 2013), 149.

132. Ibid.

133. Ibid., 150.

134. Ibid.

135. Ex. 19:3–6.

136. Also see Deut. 1; Prov. 29:2; Ro. 14:11-12; 1 Tim.3:5.

137. Ex. 20:3-17.

138. Verna M. Hall, *Teaching and Learning America's Christian History: American Revolution Bicentennial Edition* (San Francisco, CA: Foundation for American Christian Education, 1980), 158.

139. Roland de Vaux, *Ancient Israel Vol. l: Social Institutions* (New York, NY: McGraw-Hill Book Company, 1965), 143.

140. Ibid.

141. Matt. 22:37–40 RSV.

142. William Foxwell Albright, *From the Stone Age to Christianity: Monotheism and the Historical Process* (Garden City, NY: Doubleday Anchor Books, 1957), 16; 259.

143. Ibid., 258.

144. John Bright, *The Kingdom of God* (Nashville, TN: Abingdon Press, 1953), 26.

145. Ibid., 27.

146. Glenn R. Paauw, *Saving the Bible from Ourselves: Learning to Read and Live the Bible Well* (Downers Grove, IL: IVP Books, 2016), 85.

147. Ibid., 99.

148. *Teaching and Learning*, p.240.

149. Gleaves Whitney, 2007; virtual pamphlet.

150. Jon Meacham, *American Gospel: God, the Founding Fathers, and the Making of a Nation* (New York, NY: Random House Publishers, 2006), 75.

151. R. Ludwigson, *A Survey of Bible Prophecy* (Grand Rapids, MI: Zondervan Publishing House, 1974), 70.

152. Scot McKnight, *Kingdom Conspiracy: Returning to the Radical Mission of the Local Church* (Grand Rapids, MI: Brazos Press, 2014), 72.

153. Acts 17:6b–8 RSV.

154. *Kingdom Conspiracy*, 77.

155. See: Lk. 2:30–32; Matt. 10:5, 6; 15:24; Jn. 4:39-42; Ro.9:4, 5; Ro. 10:11–13.

156. *Kingdom Conspiracy*, 65–66.

157. References in this sequence were from the New Living Translation.

158. Reggie McNeal, *Kingdom Come: We Must Give Up Our Obsession with Fixing the Church—and What We Should Do Instead* (Carol Stream, IL: Tyndale Momentum, 2015), 23.

159. To read a full biography, see my book *Biblical Eldership: Back to the Future with Spirit-Filled Leadership in the Local Church.*

160. See 1 Cor.12:4–11; Ro. 12:4-8; Eph. 4:11-13.

161. I express my gratitude to Mrs. Millie Jarvis of Columbus, Ohio, for much of the inspiration for this chapter.

162. Peter Hocken, *Azusa, Rome, and Zion: Pentecostal Faith, Catholic Reform, and Jewish Roots* (Eugene, OR: Pickwick Publications, 2016), 76.

163. Ibid., 107.

164. Remarks given by Dr. Hocken at the Charismatic Leaders Fellowship, Regent University, February, 2012.

165. Empowered21 Global Council, June 2019, Bogota, Colombia.

166. Robert Morris, *Frequency: Tune In. Hear God* (Nashville, TN.: Thomas Nelson Publishers, 2016), 81.

167. Joel 3:14 RSV.

168. A complete breakdown of the movement can be accessed at All America.org.

169. Gen.22:17 RSV.

170. Rev.1:5–6 RSV.

171. Matt.25:1–13.

172. Dan Juster and Keith Intrater, *Israel, the Church, and the Last Days* (Shippensburg, PA: Destiny Image Publishers,1990), 9.

173. See Is.43:18–19.

174. R.T. Kendall, *Prepare Your Heart for the Midnight Cry: A Call to Be Ready for Christ's Return* (Lake Mary, FL: Charisma House Publishers, 2016)

175. Robert Mapes Anderson, *Vision of the Disinherited: The Making of American Pentecostalism* (Peabody, MA: Hendrickson Publishers, 1992), 96.

176. Ibid., 81.

177. Ibid., 79.

178. Ps. 130:5–6 RSV.

179. Ps. 123:2.

180. All the Scriptures in this section are from the RSV.

181. Rev. 11:1–14.

182. Kendall, *Prepare*, 85.

183. Guy Chevreau, *Catch the Fire: The Toronto Blessing* (Toronto, Canada: Harper Perennial, Harper Collins Publishers, 1995), 49.

184. Ibid.

185. Ibid.

186. Lk. 4:21.

187. Lk. 10:24 RSV.

188. John C. Lennox, *Against the Flow: The Inspiration of Daniel in an Age of Relativism* (Oxford, UK: Monarch Books, 2015), 326.

189. RSV.

190. George Otis Jr.: *Can America Vote Its Way to National Health? Part lll*, 28 October 2020, The Sentinel Group.

191. Joel 3:14.

192. Phil. 2:12–13 RSV.

193. 2 Thess. 2:8 RSV.

194. See 1 Ki. 18:46 RSV

195. J.I. Packer, Merrill C. Tenney, William White, Jr., *The Bible Almanac: A Comprehensive Handbook of the People of the Bible and How they Lived* (Nashville, TN: Thomas Nelson Publishers, 1980), 71.

196. From the movie in 1956 *The Man Who Knew Too Much* when Doris Day won an Academy Award for Best Music (Original Song).

197. Col. 1:16–17.

198. Joshua 1.

199. 2 Ki. 6:11.

200. Heb. 12:2.

201. Eph.1:18; Job 42:1-5.

202. Ps. 123:1 RSV.

203. Matt. 6:22.

204. Ps. 119:18 RSV.

205. Jn. 5:24. Also see 1 Cor. 2:9; Ezek. 33:3; Deut. 30:11ff; Acts 28:26.

206. Ro. 4:17 KJV.

207. 2 Chron. 16:9.

208. See Jer. 32:17; Mk. 10:27.

209. Jn. 14:12. NLT.

210. Mk. 11:23–24.

211. 1 Thess. 5:4.

212. Lev. 6:8–13.

213. Gary T. Amos, *Defending the Declaration: How the Bible and Christianity Influenced the Writing of the Declaration of Independence* (Brentwood, TN: Wolgemuth & Hyatt Publishers, Inc., 1989), 3.

214. *American Heritage Dictionary*, 1970 ed., s.v. "Deism."

215. Carl Becker, *The Declaration of Independence: A Study in the History of Political Ideas* (New York, NY: Vintage Books, 1958), 37.

216. Ibid.

217. *Defending the Declaration*, 39.

218. Revised Standard Translation.

219. John Locke, *An Essay Concerning Human Understanding*, 2 Vols., ed. Alexander Campbell Fraser (New York, NY: Dover Publications, 1959), Vol. 1, Prolegomena.

220. David Barton, *Original Intent: The Courts, The Constitution, and Religion* (Aledo, TX: Fifth Printing, February 2013), 225.

221. *The Reasonableness of Christianity* (1696) and *A Vindication of the Reasonableness of Christianity* (1697).

222. *Defending the Declaration*, 54.

223. *Original Intent*, 59.

224. Sydney E. Ahlstrom, *A Religious History of the American People* (New Haven, CT: Yale University Press, 1972), 366.

225. *Defending*, 75.

226. Ibid.

227. Ibid., 77.

228. Ibid., 78.

229. Ibid.

230. Ibid., 83.

231. Ibid., 80.

232. *Defending*, 104. Note: The Declaration uses the word "unalienable," however, there is an alternative spelling of "inalienable," which means the exact same thing.

233. Gen. 18:25 (RSV).

234. See also 2 Sam. 15:4; 2 Chron. 6:35, 39; Job 13:18, 23:4, 31:13; and Is. 50:8.

235. See also 1 Ki. 8:45, 49; Job 34:6, 36:6; Ps.9:4, 140:12; Jer. 5:28, 32:7–8; Lam. 3:35; and Ezek. 21:27.

236. *Defending*, p. 110.

237. Matt. 5:3–12.

238. *Defending*, 128.

239. Ibid., 131.

240. Ibid., 132.

241. 2 Ki. 11

242. 2 Chron. 23:12.

243. The Declaration of Independence.

244. Gary T. Amos, *Defending the Declaration: How the Bible and Christianity Influenced the Writing of the Declaration of Independence* (Brentwood, TN: Wolgemuth & Hyatt Publishers, Inc., 1989), 3.

245. All scripture from Appendix B are from the Revised Standard Version of the Bible.

246. Is. 58:9.

247. Mk. 9:23–29.

248. Tyson, p.1; *Way of the Wesley's*, Christian History Magazine, #132.

249. S.P.E.C. is the oldest Anglican mission agency in the world, dating from 1698, led by Thomas Bray.

250. The Holy Club by Charles J. Little; Nov.30, 1907/ Encyclopedia Britannica, Ton to Zym.

251. See Matt. 28:16–29.

252. See Eph. 4:17–20.

CPSIA information can be obtained
at www.ICGtesting.com
Printed in the USA
LVHW110014261021
701552LV00003B/72